The Developing Child
Student Activity Manual

 **Glencoe**

New York, New York   Columbus, Ohio   Chicago, Illinois   Peoria, Illinois   Woodland Hills, California

The **McGraw-Hill** Companies

Send all inquiries to:
Glencoe/McGraw-Hill
3008 W. Willow Knolls Drive
Peoria, IL 61614-1083

ISBN 0-07-868970-8 (Student Activity Manual)

Printed in the United States of America
2 3 4 5 6 7 8 9   009   09 08 07 06 05

TABLE OF CONTENTS

Table of Contents

Table of Contents

Unit 5: The Child from Four to Six

Chapter 13: Physical Development from Four to Six

Chapter 14: Emotional and Social Development from Four to Six

Chapter 15: Intellectual Development from Four to Six

Unit 6: The Child from Seven to Twelve

Chapter 16: Physical Development from Seven to Twelve

Chapter 17: Emotional and Social Development from Seven to Twelve

Chapter 18: Intellectual Development from Seven to Twelve

TABLE OF CONTENTS

Unit 7: Additional Topics of Study

Chapter 19: Adolescence

Chapter 20: Children's Health and Safety

Chapter 21: Family Challenges

Chapter 22: Child Care and Early Education

Chapter 23: Careers Working with Children

Learning About Children **CHAPTER 1**

Study Guide

> **Directions:** Answer the following questions as you read the chapter. They will help you focus on the main points. Later, you can use this guide to review and study the chapter information.

Section 1-1: Making a Difference in Children's Lives

1. Identify four ways you can benefit from studying children. _____
   _____
   _____
   _____

2. What are *typical behaviors*? How can knowing about them help you better understand children's behavior?
   _____
   _____

3. Identify four things that *caregivers* provide to children, in addition to food and clothes. _____
   _____
   _____
   _____

4. Compare the lives of children today with those in the 1800s in the areas of health, education, and work.
   _____
   _____
   _____
   _____

5. Why is play important to children? _____

6. How might studying about children affect your views of childhood? _____
   _____
   _____

(Continued on next page)

Section 1-2: Studying Children

7. How developed is a baby's brain at birth? How does it change by age three? _____

_____

_____

_____

8. How does *stimulation* help a baby develop? _____

_____

_____

_____

9. How does living in a stimulating *environment* affect neural pathways in the brain as a child matures?

_____

_____

_____

10. Briefly summarize the main findings of each of the following child development theorists.

A. Freud: _____

_____

B. Piaget: _____

_____

C. Vygotsky: _____

_____

D. Erikson: _____

_____

E. Skinner: _____

_____

F. Bandura: _____

_____

G. Bronfenbrenner: _____

_____

(Continued on next page)

Learning About Children   *Chapter 1 continued*

11. Explain in your own words what the following characteristics of development mean.

A. Development is similar for each individual. _____

_____

_____

B. Development builds on earlier learning. _____

_____

_____

C. Development proceeds at an individual rate. _____

_____

_____

D. The different areas of development are interrelated. _____

_____

E. Development is a lifelong process. _____

_____

_____

12. Name two major influences on development and give an example of each. _____

_____

_____

13. What are typical *developmental tasks* of the following stages of the *human life cycle*?

A. Adolescence: _____

_____

B. Young adulthood: _____

_____

C. The Thirties: _____

_____

_____

D. Middle age: _____

_____

_____

E. Late adulthood: _____

_____

_____

F. Very late adulthood: _____

_____

_____

(Continued on next page)

14. Describe how *self-esteem* affects development. _____

_____

_____

_____

_____

15. Give three examples of ways parents and other caregivers can help children develop self-esteem.

_____

_____

_____

_____

Section 1-3: Observing and Interacting with Children

16. What are the benefits of observing children? _____

_____

_____

_____

17. How are *objective* observations different from *subjective* observations? _____

_____

_____

18. Which type of observation do you think is more useful, objective or subjective? Why?

_____

_____

_____

19. Describe each type of observation record, and explain when to use it.

A. *Running record:* _____

_____

_____

_____

B. *Anecdotal record:* _____

_____

_____

_____

(Continued on next page)

Learning About Children   ***Chapter 1 continued***

    C. *Frequency count:* _____

_____

_____

_____

    D. *Developmental checklist:* _____

_____

_____

_____

20. When doing a frequency count, why is it important to first establish a baseline count?

_____

_____

_____

_____

_____

21. How should you position yourself and interact with children when observing? _____

_____

_____

_____

22. Derrick is observing a specific child. What kinds of data about the child should he record in his notes?

_____

_____

_____

_____

23. What is the difference between observation and *interpretation*? _____

_____

_____

_____

24. Explain the importance of confidentiality in connection with observation records. _____

_____

_____

_____

_____

_____

Name _____ Date _____ Class _____

Making a Difference in Children's Lives

Thinking About Children

Directions: Complete the following sentences about children. There are no right answers. When you complete all questions, reread your answers. What do they tell you about your attitudes about children?

1. Studying about children can help me … _____
_____

2. What I like most about children is … _____
_____

3. What I like least about children is … _____
_____

4. My favorite activity as a child was … _____
_____

5. Children learn best by … _____
_____

6. Children need parents or other caregivers because … _____
_____

7. If I were a parent, I would … _____
_____

8. Most of my knowledge of children has come from … _____
_____

9. All children are alike in that they … _____
_____

10. All children are different in that they … _____
_____

11. One of the hardest things for a child to learn is … _____
_____

12. The greatest challenge in caring for a child is … _____
_____

13. I don't understand why children … _____
_____

14. The first thing that comes to mind when I think of a newborn is … _____
_____

(Continued on next page)

12   The Developing Child: **Student Activity Manual**

Copyright © Glencoe/McGraw-Hill,
a division of The McGraw-Hill Companies, Inc.

Making a Difference in Children's Lives

15. My favorite age of children is ... _____
_____

16. When I am with children, I am surprised by... _____
_____

17. A major goal of a child care center should be ... _____
_____

18. One thing I hope to learn in this class is ... _____
_____

19. Reread your answers in this activity. Then describe what your answers reveal about your attitudes toward children.

_____
_____
_____
_____
_____
_____

20. Do you think a career related to children might interest you? Why or why not?

_____
_____
_____
_____
_____
_____

Studying Children

Describing Development

Directions: Review the characteristics of development in the box below. Then read each situation and identify the characteristic(s) of development. Write the appropriate characteristic or characteristics in the answer spaces.

Characteristics of Development
- Development is similar for everyone.
- Development builds on earlier learning.
- Development proceeds at an individual rate.
- The different areas of development are interrelated.
- Development continues throughout life.

---

1. Sarah lives in a home with her parents, a brother and sister, and her grandparents. Her grandparents are now retired from working. They help watch the younger children while Sarah's parents are at work.

   _____

   _____

2. In school, Michael did poorly on tests and was seldom able to answer the teacher's question. Other children teased him and called him names. As a result, he was shy and had little self-confidence. He recently started wearing glasses and, since he can see the board more clearly, is doing better in school. He feels more positive about himself and is now getting along better with the other children.

   _____

3. Josh and Nicole are cousins. Although Josh is two months older, Nicole began to sit and stand at about the same time he did.

   _____

   _____

4. Chris was looking at the pictures in the family photo album. He saw photos of his daughter Ally when she was an infant and started lifting herself on her arms and legs. About a month later, she began crawling, and then stood up while holding on to furniture. Now Ally moves about the room by "cruising"—walking while touching furniture.

   _____

   _____

(Continued on next page)

Studying Children

5. Erin and her family spent the summer visiting relatives in Toronto. Erin helped the parents by watching her sister Michelle and cousin Brian, both two years old. She noticed that both children could run fairly well, stand on one foot, and climb stairs. They both enjoyed playing with sand and liked finger painting.

_____

_____

6. Emma, Rachel, and Juan all attend the same child care center. Emma is slightly shorter than the other two. She enjoys being with others and plays well with others. Rachel is the tallest and most coordinated. She tends to stay near the center's workers and spends little time with the children. Juan is of average size. He plays quietly by himself although he joins in group activities when they are scheduled.

_____

_____

_____

7. Jessica is an active three-year-old. Lately, she has started choosing her clothes each morning. Her parents are amazed at her eagerness to learn new things—it seems she never stops wanting to learn.

_____

_____

_____

8. Luke is helping his younger brother Drew learn the alphabet. Drew seems to be catching on very quickly. Yesterday, he called out some of the letters on a store sign as he and Luke walked down the street. Luke knows that soon Drew will be able to point out a few simple words and not long after that he'll be reading sentences.

_____

_____

_____

9. Jeremy is observing the activities of a group of two-year-olds at a child care center. He notes that Heather can now stack six blocks before her tower collapses. Last month, her maximum was five blocks. Joey's tower tends to topple after the fourth block.

_____

_____

_____

10. Sam was not very good at kickball. He was smaller than other children his age and not as strong. When he failed to kick the ball well, he often lost interest and left the game. He preferred to sit quietly with a book instead of playing outside. Soon, his reading skills surpassed those of the other children in his class.

_____

_____

Observing and Interacting with Children   **SECTION 1–3**

Interpreting Observations

> **Directions:** Read the following notes that one student wrote while observing children in a preschool. In the space below, write your interpretation of children's behavior, based on the notes.

Brett alone in block area. Putting blocks together on the floor. Object he's making gets wider, taller.
Tomas comes to area, asked what **Brett** was doing.
Brett: "I'm making a space station."
Tomas picks up some stray blocks. Begins to place them in new combination to right of **Brett.** "Here's a ship from Mars."
Brett: "No, that's not where it comes in." Stopped working and stood with hands on hips.
Tomas: "This is the Mars space mission coming back to report. There's a big meeting on the station 'cuz…'cuz…there's a monster in space that's gonna eat the Mars colony."
Colin arrives. Watches others. "What're you playing?"
Brett doesn't answer. Shakes head at **Tomas** "No monsters. They can't live in space." Kneels, looking at a block. "It's an asteroid that's heading to Mars."
Tomas nods. Speaks quickly. "Yeah. It's a big asteroid that's going to hit the colony on Mars. It's going to destroy everything. They need help."
Brett picks up other block. Moves it through air, making engine sounds. Walks around area. Steps over and around blocks that are part of game. "Here's the president of the earth. He's coming to the meeting to decide what to do."
Colin: "Can I play?"
Brett: "You can be the Admiral. You command the space force. Come to the meeting too."
Tomas moves to other area. Clears stray blocks off floor. Puts blocks together making buildings. "Here's the Mars colony." Takes smaller blocks. Moves them from ground to air. "People are leaving. They're afraid."
Colin takes block and moves it through air. "The scout goes out to watch the asteroid. The crew has to see what it looks like."

_____

_____

_____

_____

_____

_____

_____

_____

The Challenges of Parenting

CHAPTER 2

Study Guide

> **Directions:** Answer the following questions as you read the chapter. They will help you focus on the main points. Later, you can use this guide to review and study the chapter information.

Section 2–1: Parenting and Families?

1. Give a brief definition of *parenting*. _____
_____

2. Describe three actions you could take to make a positive difference in a child's life. _____
_____
_____
_____
_____

3. How can it help parents to learn about child development? _____
_____
_____
_____

4. Describe four actions you could take to help build your parenting skills. _____
_____
_____
_____
_____

5. For the parenting tasks described below, indicate the correct order and then identify the stage and time period (ages of children) for each, according to Galinsky's model.

_____ A. Determine rules: _____

_____ B. Establish boundaries: _____

_____ C. Begin to imagine yourself as a parent: _____

_____ D. Evaluate your parenting: _____

_____ E. Become emotionally attached to your child: _____

_____ F. Decide what knowledge, skills, and values your child needs: _____
_____

(Continued on next page)

6. Describe at least three ways new parents' lifestyles often change. _____

_____

_____

_____

_____

7. Why might a new parent experience some negative emotions? _____

_____

_____

_____

8. When new parents feel overwhelmed, they may argue with one another. Describe how they can get past such trouble spots.

_____

_____

_____

_____

9. What are some of the rewards of parenthood? _____

_____

_____

_____

_____

10. Explain in your own words why each of the following considerations is important to the decision of whether to have children.

A. *Emotional maturity:* _____

_____

_____

B. Desire for parenthood: _____

_____

_____

C. Health: _____

_____

_____

_____

(Continued on next page)

The Challenges of Parenting   *Chapter 2 continued*

    D. Financial concerns: _____

_____

_____

_____

    E. Resource management: _____

_____

_____

_____

11. Give an example of a family goal that would require parents to use good resource management skills.

_____

_____

_____

_____

Section 2–2: Teen Parenthood

12. What is *sexuality*? _____

_____

_____

13. How do *hormones* affect teens? _____

_____

14. What personal values might a teen use to help make responsible decisions about sexual activity?

_____

_____

_____

15. What is a *sexually transmitted disease (STD)*? Identify three possible serious effects of STDs.

_____

_____

_____

16. What is the only guaranteed way to prevent STDs and pregnancy? _____

_____

17. Identify four medical problems for which teen mothers are at high risk? _____

_____

(Continued on next page)

18. Why should teen parents make graduating from high school a high-priority goal? _____

_____

_____

19. Why is it especially important to establish *paternity* when parents do not marry? _____

_____

_____

20. How might relationships with friends change for teens who become parents? _____

_____

_____

21. When teens marry because of pregnancy, what challenge do they face in addition to the challenges of marriage?

_____

_____

22. What special challenges do teens who are single parents face? _____

_____

_____

_____

23. Describe two types of adoption. _____

_____

_____

_____

_____

Parenting and Families

Resource Management Skills

Directions: Good resource management involves five key steps. Read each situation described below. In the middle column, indicate which step in the management process the situation involves. In the right column, indicate whether or not you think the person is acting wisely and explain your reasoning. After analyzing these situations, answer Question 7 on the next page.

Steps in Resource Management

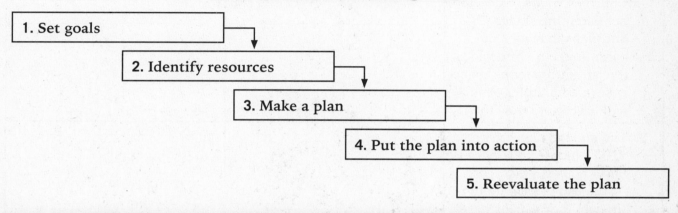

1. Set goals
2. Identify resources
3. Make a plan
4. Put the plan into action
5. Reevaluate the plan

Situation	Step Involved	Your Evaluation
1. When Sarah discovers she is pregnant, she promises herself that she will complete high school with the rest of her class.		
2. Todd is having difficulty with math. He thinks he can get help from his older brother or from his mother, who is an engineer.		

(Continued on next page)

Situation	Step Involved	Your Evaluation
3. Brandon decided to leave school when his girlfriend became pregnant. His new job, though, pays too little to support his new family. He is looking into other options, such as taking classes at night to get his diploma.		
4. Courtney wants to develop her parenting skills. She plans to read about parenting, but she decides to wait until after her baby is born. She thinks she will have more time then.		
5. Tim and Jan plan to save $100 a month so they can buy a house in five years. At the end of each month, though, they usually have no money left over to save. "That's okay. We'll make up for it next month," Tim says.		
6. Kelly wants to find the right child care center for her son. She checks the phone book for centers in her area and asks for recommendations from friends.		

7. Describe a situation in which a teen might improve the situation by using these steps.

_____

_____

_____

_____

_____

_____

_____

Name _____ Date _____ Class _____

Teen Parenthood

SECTION 2–2

Adjusting to Parenthood

Directions: Read the following situation, and then answer the questions that follow. Write your answers in the spaces provided.

Cassie had trouble keeping her attention on her driving. Her stomach was still tight, something she always felt after dropping off her month-old baby Nathan at her mother's house. Cassie desperately needed the income from her job, but she felt it was still too soon to leave her son in someone else's care, even her mother's. She was miserable.

Cassie discovered she was pregnant in March of her senior year in high school. She graduated, then married Tim in June. Their life had been stressful. Tim was working two part-time minimum wage jobs, but it just wasn't enough. Cassie's doctor was concerned about both Cassie and the baby and told her she had to stay in bed most of the time. Nathan was born three weeks early, small but healthy.

Without medical insurance, the bills for prenatal care and the baby's birth seemed overwhelming. Cassie knew she needed to get a job. When her mother volunteered to care for Nathan, it was a big relief. She knew he would be well cared for and they wouldn't have to pay child care fees. Her job as a receptionist didn't pay a lot, but it did come with medical insurance.

Cassie worried constantly about missing Nathan and their debts. She and Tim hardly seemed to see each other because of their work schedules. She found herself making silly mistakes at work because she had difficulty concentrating. Now she was afraid she might be fired. "Pull yourself together," she whispered to herself as she pulled into the parking lot at work.

1. How may Cassie's relationship with her mother be changing? _____

_____

_____

_____

_____

_____

_____

_____

(Continued on next page)

Copyright © Glencoe/McGraw-Hill
a division of The McGraw-Hill Companies, Inc.

The Developing Child: **Student Activity Manual**   23

2. What impact is the birth of her baby having on Cassie's career? _____

_____

_____

_____

_____

_____

3. Why do you think Cassie is experiencing so much doubt and anxiety? _____

_____

_____

_____

_____

_____

4. How do you think their financial situation may affect Cassie and Tim's marriage?

_____

_____

_____

_____

_____

_____

5. Both Tim and Cassie had planned to continue their education. What are the chances of doing so now? What are likely to be the consequences of not doing so?

_____

_____

_____

_____

_____

_____

Name _____ Date _____ Class _____

Building Strong Families

CHAPTER 3

Study Guide

> **Directions:** Answer the following questions as you read the chapter. They will help you focus on the main points. Later, you can use this guide to review and study the chapter information.

Section 3–1: Families: The Context for Parenting

1. What are two main functions that families perform? _____
   _____
   _____
   _____

2. For each basic need listed below, give one example of how families meet that need for their children.
   A. Physical: _____
   _____
   _____

   B. Emotional: _____
   _____
   _____

   C. Social: _____
   _____
   _____

   D. Intellectual: _____
   _____
   _____

3. How do families pass on values? _____
   _____
   _____

4. Give an example of each of the following types of family structures.
   A. *Nuclear family:* _____
   B. *Single-parent family:* _____
   C. *Blended family:* _____
   D. *Extended family:* _____

5. After his parents divorced, Ryan lived with his mother. In this case, who was Ryan's *custodial parent*—his father or his mother?
   _____

(Continued on next page)

6. Name and describe three ways that a child may join a family other than as the family's biological child.

_____

_____

_____

_____

_____

_____

_____

7. Describe the following stages of the family life cycle.

A. Beginning Stage: _____

_____

_____

B. Parental Stage 1: _____

_____

_____

C. Parental Stage 2: _____

_____

_____

D. Parental Stage 3: _____

_____

_____

E. Middle Age: _____

_____

_____

_____

F. Retirement: _____

_____

_____

(Continued on next page)

Name _____ Date _____ Class _____

8. Read the following account of one family. Then, in the lines that follow, identify at lease four trends that are affecting this family. Describe what consequences each trend might have on their lives.

> Jack and Amber Henderson just moved from the West coast to the East. All other family members still live in the West, except Jack's mother, who has come to live with them. The family moved because Jack's company transferred him. The transfer came with a promotion and raise. Amber is pregnant with their third child. She works at home, communicating with her customers by e-mail and fax.

_____

_____

_____

_____

_____

_____

_____

9. Identify three sources of support available to families under stress. _____

_____

_____

10. How does spending time together help to build strong families? _____

_____

_____

11. Name one value that a family may share. _____

12. Identify three ways families can handle conflict. _____

_____

Section 3–2: Effective Parenting Skills

13. Name and describe three categories of children's needs. _____

_____

_____

_____

(Continued on next page)

14. How are children affected by *deprivation?* _____

_____

_____

15. Identify the *parenting style* described in each situation below.

    A. Zoe was playing ball in the house, which was against the rules. When she broke a lamp, her mother asked Zoe what punishment she should receive.

    _____

    B. Shauna did not take out the trash as she was instructed to do, and her father scolded her quickly and firmly.

    _____

    C. When Jeff drew pictures on his bedroom wall, his parents ignored it._____

    _____

16. Describe three outcomes of effective guidance. _____

_____

_____

_____

_____

17. Identify and give an example of three basic ways that parents can encourage appropriate behavior.

_____

_____

_____

_____

_____

_____

_____

18. How does setting limits help children grow into responsible adults? _____

_____

_____

19. What three questions should parents consider in setting limits? _____

_____

_____

_____

_____

(Continued on next page)

Building Strong Families

20. When thinking about how to respond to misbehavior, what three questions should caregivers consider?

_____

_____

_____

_____

_____

21. What message should caregivers convey when they punish a child? _____

_____

_____

_____

22. For each situation described below, identify the method of *negative reinforcement* used.

A. Sam loved to go to the park. When he continued to break the rule about not riding his scooter in the street, his father told him that they would not go to the park that day.

_____

B. In spite of her mother's warning, Carley jumped on her favorite toy and broke it. Her mother did not replace the toy. Carley had to do without it.

_____

C. When Joey continued to hit other children after repeated warnings, the preschool teacher instructed him to sit in the "quiet chair" for five minutes.

_____

D. Jacob's mother told Jacob to stop running his toy truck into his sister. When he continued, she told him that she was taking his truck away for the day.

_____

23. Name a poor disciplinary method and explain why it is not effective. _____

_____

_____

_____

_____

24. Why is consistency important when guiding children's behavior? _____

_____

_____

_____

_____

Families: The Context for Parenting

Families Today

Directions: Read each description of a family. Then identify the family structure and the trend affecting the family by writing your responses in the appropriate box.

Description	Family Structure	Trend
The Michelsons family includes a father, a mother, and one child from the mother's previous marriage. Both parents work from offices in the family home.		
Pete Washburn won custody of his two children when he and his wife divorced. He works two jobs to earn extra money.		
Aberto and Anamaria Nuñez have two children. They have moved three times over a 20-year period.		
The Iversons married when they were 20 and have three children. Recently, they brought Erik Iverson's mother to live with them because she is no longer able to care for herself.		
Sue Watson is raising her daughter on her own. She and her daughter had to move to another town so she could keep her job.		

Name _____ Date _____ Class _____

Effective Parenting Skills

Evaluating Guidance Techniques

Directions: Effective guidance helps children learn to get along with others and deal with their own feelings. The following situations show caregivers trying to guide children's behavior. If the method they used was effective, write **Yes** in the right-hand column. If not, write **No**. In the space below each situation, explain why or why not.

Situation	Effective?
1. Seth described to his father how he and his friends had made fun of a new student. His father laughed at the names they had called the new girl. Then he said, "You really should be nicer to her."	
2. Jasmine and Kiesha were playing in the living room. As their voices grew louder, Kiesha's mother came to the door of the room and said, "Girls, I'm glad you're having a good time, but you are so loud you are going to wake the baby up. Would you like to play outside, where you can be noisy, or do you want to play more quietly in here?"	
3. When Chase's father got home from work, he discovered the crayon drawings that Chase had made all over his bedroom walls. The father made Chase promise to "never do anything like this again."	

(Continued on next page)

Situation	Effective?
4. Amy Wong saw her eleven-month-old reaching for the electric socket. Amy said "No!" very sharply and came over to the baby. She pointed to the socket and said, "That's a no-no. You cannot touch that." Then she picked the baby up, saying "Let's look at a book now."	
5. Tommy was pushing his vegetable around on his plate. His mother said, "Look, if you eat your broccoli, you can have some ice cream."	
6. It was a rainy day. Damen and Brooke, both preschoolers, had been bickering. When Damen objected to something Brooke called him, he smacked her on the arm. When Brooke complained, he did it again. Brooke hit Damen back just as their mother entered the room. She quickly gave Brooke time-out for hitting.	
7. Tory found three-year-old Jake digging in the flower bed. He had already dug up one plant and was walking with his shovel toward another. Tory grasped his hand and began to lead him to the sandbox, saying, "We dig in the sandbox, not in the garden. If we dig up the plants, we won't have any flowers. If you want to dig, you can dig in the sand."	

Prenatal Development

CHAPTER 4

Study Guide

> **Directions:** Answer the following questions as you read the chapter. They will help you focus on the main points. Later, you can use this guide to review and study the chapter information.

Section 4–1: The Developing Baby

1. Briefly summarize the process of *conception*. Use the following terms in your summary: *Fallopian tube, uterus, sperm, ovum.*

   _____

   _____

   _____

2. Complete the following chart about the stages of *prenatal development.*

Stage	Time Span	Development That Occurs
	Conception to two weeks	
	Third through eighth week	
	Eighth or ninth week through birth	

3. Explain what each of the following is and describe the functions each performs.

   A. *Amniotic fluid:* _____

   _____

   B. *Placenta:* _____

   _____

   C. *Umbilical cord:* _____

   _____

(Continued on next page)

4. Briefly summarize the changes that commonly occur in a woman during the first two months of pregnancy.

_____

_____

_____

5. What is "lightening" and when does it occur? _____

_____

_____

Section 4–2: A Closer Look at Conception

6. What is heredity? Name three characteristics that can be hereditary. _____

_____

_____

_____

7. Summarize the relationship between *chromosomes, genes, genomes,* and *DNA.* _____

_____

_____

_____

_____

8. Explain the difference between *dominant genes* and *recessive genes.* _____

_____

_____

_____

9. Which parent can provide either an X or Y chromosome to the baby? Which chromosome must come from this parent for the child to be female?

_____

10. Explain how each of the following occurs:

   A. Identical twins: _____

   _____

   B. Fraternal twins: _____

   _____

11. What is the only guaranteed way to avoid pregnancy? _____

(Continued on next page)

   The Developing Child: **Student Activity Manual**   Copyright © Glencoe/McGraw-Hill,
a division of The McGraw-Hill Companies, Inc.

Prenatal Development

12. Complete the following chart about options for *infertility*.

Options	Description
Adoption	
	Sperm is injected into a woman's uterus.
	An egg from the woman is removed and fertilized with sperm from the man and then placed in the woman's uterus.
Ovum transfer	
Surrogate mother	

13. What are two reasons a couple who want children might not use these options? _____

_____

Section 4–3: Problems in Prenatal Development

14. Explain the difference between a *miscarriage* and a *stillbirth*. _____

_____

15. Identify each *birth defect* described below.

A. Inability of body to process a common protein: _____

B. Malformed red blood cells interfere with oxygen supply: _____

C. Lack of a certain blood chemical makes body unable to process certain fats in the brain and nerve cells:

_____

D. Extra chromosome 21 typically results in mental retardation: _____

16. Describe the causes of birth defects within each category listed below.

A. Environment: _____

_____

B. Heredity: _____

_____

C. Errors in chromosomes: _____

_____

D. Interaction of heredity and environment: _____

_____

_____

(Continued on next page)

The Developing Child: **Student Activity Manual**

17. What does a genetic counselor do? _____

_____

18. Complete the following chart about prenatal tests.

Prenatal Test	Description	Risk
Alpha-fetoprotein (AFP)		No known risk
	Sound waves are used to make a video image of the unborn baby.	
Amniocentesis		
Chorionic villi sampling		

Section 4–4: Avoiding Dangers to the Baby

19. Compare *fetal alcohol syndrome (FAS)* and *fetal alcohol effects*. How are they similar? How are they different?

_____

_____

_____

20. Why is it critical to avoid taking medications in the first three months of pregnancy unless specifically prescribed?

_____

_____

_____

21. Describe the possible effects on a baby of each hazard listed below.

A. Caffeine: _____

_____

B. Tobacco: _____

_____

C. Cocaine: _____

_____

_____

(Continued on next page)

Prenatal Development

22. What is *SIDS*? _____

_____

23. If an expectant mother needs X rays because of an accident, why should she tell the doctors that she is pregnant?

_____

_____

24. Give three examples of hazardous substances pregnant women should avoid. _____

_____

25. Complete the following chart about infections during pregnancy.

Infection	Possible Effects on Baby	Prevention
Rubella		
Toxoplasmosis		
Chicken pox		
STDs	Serious illnesses, physical disabilities, death	
AIDS		

Name _____ Date _____ Class _____

The Developing Baby

Stages of Prenatal Development

Directions: Each letter in the lists below describes what happens at a particular time during a baby's prenatal development or a mother's pregnancy. For each description, write the month of pregnancy in which it typically occurs.

Developing Baby

A. Moves into head-down position. _____

B. Internal organs begin to form. _____

C. Fetus is about 3 inches long. _____

D. All organs are present but immature. _____

E. Breathing movements begin. _____

F. Fetus acquires antibodies from mother. _____

G. Bones begin to form. _____

Mother

H. Breasts begin to swell. _____

I. Lightening felt. _____

J. Strong fetal movements. _____

K. Appetite increases. _____

L. Missed menstrual period. _____

M. Possible backache, shortness of breath, fatigue. _____

N. Uterus is about the size of an orange. _____

Directions: Use the answers above to complete the time lines on the next page. Arrange the descriptions of a baby's prenatal development and a mother's pregnancy in the correct sequence from conception to birth. Write the letter of the earliest event in the circle in the top box and note the event. Continue until the time lines for both the baby and mother are completed.

(Continued on next page)

Developing Baby

Development and Pregnancy Time Line

BABY		MOTHER
CONCEPTION		
○		○
○		○
END OF MONTH 2		
○		○
○		○
END OF MONTH 4		
○		○
END OF MONTH 6		
○		○
END OF MONTH 8		
○		○

Name _____ Date _____ Class _____

A Closer Look at Conception

Heredity in the Works

> **Directions:** Fill in the grid for each situation to determine the chances the couple has of passing on the genetic trait described. Then complete the statements that follow, summarizing your findings.

1. The woman is blue-eyed and carries two genes for blue eyes. The man is brown-eyed and carries one gene for brown eyes and one gene for blue eyes. Complete the grid to determine the chances that any child they have will be born with blue or brown eyes.

Mother

Father

	b	b
B		
b		

> **B** = the gene for brown eyes (dominant)
> **b** = the gene for blue eyes (recessive)

   A. There is a _____ in _____ chance that any child will have brown eyes and carry genes for both brown and blue eyes.

   B. There is a _____ in _____ chance that any child will have blue eyes and carry genes for blue eyes only.

2. The mother and father both carry a gene for sickle cell anemia, a disease caused by having two recessive genes. They do not have the disease but may pass it on to their children. Complete the grid to determine the chances that any child will be born with the disease.

Mother

Father

	r	n
r		
n		

> **r** = a gene that carries the recessive trait for sickle cell anemia
> **n** = a normal gene without the sickle cell trait

   A. There is a _____ in _____ chance that any child will have sickle cell anemia and carry two genes for it.

   B. There is a _____ in _____ chance that any child will carry a gene for sickle cell anemia but not have the disease.

   C. There is a _____ in _____ chance that any child will not have sickle cell anemia or carry a gene for it.

Problems in Prenatal Development

Detecting Birth Defects

Directions: Match the symptoms in the left-hand column to the birth defects listed in the right-hand column. Write the letter of the correct answer in the blank to the left of each symptom.

Symptom	Birth Defect
_____ 1. Gap in roof of the mouth	**A.** Hydrocephalus
_____ 2. Progressive weakness and shrinking of the muscles	**B.** Muscular dystrophy
_____ 3. Overly rapid growth of the head	**C.** Cerebral palsy
_____ 4. Very salty sweat and a cough that doesn't go away	**D.** PKU
_____ 5. Child slow to develop motor skills	**E.** Sickle cell anemia
_____ 6. Incompletely formed spinal cord	**F.** Down syndrome
_____ 7. Tiredness, lack of appetite, and pain	**G.** Cleft palate
	H. Cystic fibrosis
	I. Spina bifida

Directions: In the diagram below, write the name of the prenatal test in the box with its description.

Tests amniotic fluid:

Tests blood for abnormal levels of a protein:

Prenatal Tests

Test that uses sound waves:

Tests tissues:

Name _____ Date _____ Class _____

Avoiding Dangers to the Baby

Facing Issues of Prenatal Care

Directions: Read the following descriptions of behavior by women who are pregnant. Decide whether the behavior is appropriate or inappropriate and place a check (✓) in the appropriate space. Then, using the spaces that follow, explain why you answered as you did.

1. Miranda suspected that she might be pregnant so she took a home pregnancy test, which confirmed that she was. A friend has told her to see a doctor, but Miranda says she can't afford it now.

   _____ **Appropriate**   _____ **Inappropriate**

   Explain your answer: _____

   _____

   _____

   _____

2. Alberto and Diane, parents of a healthy eight-year old, want another child. There is a history of birth defects in Diane's family. They are going to visit with a genetic counselor.

   _____ **Appropriate**   _____ **Inappropriate**

   Explain your answer: _____

   _____

   _____

   _____

3. Amy is a healthy twenty-three-year-old. She has just found out she's pregnant. Her best friend's baby was born with spina bifida. Amy is afraid that her child may be born with some birth defect and requests having special prenatal tests.

   _____ **Appropriate**   _____ **Inappropriate**

   Explain your answer: _____

   _____

   _____

   _____

4. Chantal and her husband Charles want to have a baby. Since they made this decision, they both have quit smoking.

   _____ **Appropriate**   _____ **Inappropriate**

   Explain your answer: _____

   _____

   _____

   _____

Name _____ Date _____ Class _____

Preparing for Birth

CHAPTER 5

Study Guide

> **Directions.** Answer the following questions as you read the chapter. They will help you focus on the main points. Later, you can use this guide to review and study the chapter information.

Section 5–1: A Healthy Pregnancy

1. Identify six common signs of pregnancy. Which is usually first? _____
   _____
   _____
   _____

2. What type of doctor specializes in pregnancy and childbirth? _____

3. Why is it important for a pregnant woman to receive regular medical care throughout her pregnancy?
   _____
   _____

4. What is *anemia*, and what are its symptoms? _____
   _____
   _____

5. Why is it important for a pregnant woman to be tested for the *Rh factor*? _____
   _____
   _____
   _____

6. How is the due date calculated? _____
   _____
   _____

7. What is *gestational diabetes*, and how can it be controlled? _____
   _____
   _____

8. What are the symptoms of *preeclampsia*, and what danger does it pose to the baby? _____
   _____
   _____

(Continued on next page)

The Developing Child: **Student Activity Manual**

9. List four discomforts that commonly occur during pregnancy. _____

_____

_____

_____

10. Explain the importance of each of the following nutrients during pregnancy.

   A. Protein: _____

   B. Folic acid: _____

   C. Vitamin A: _____

   D. Vitamin B: _____

   E. Vitamin C: _____

   _____

   F. Vitamin D: _____

   G. Iron: _____

   _____

   H. Calcium and phosphorus: _____

   _____

11. Why is it important for pregnant women to include leafy green vegetables and oranges in their diet?

_____

_____

12. Why do pregnant teens have special nutritional needs? What two nutrients are especially important for them?

_____

_____

_____

13. Why does eating cultured yogurt help some people with *lactose intolerance*? _____

_____

_____

_____

14. Lila is pregnant. About how much weight should she expect to gain during her pregnancy?

_____

15. Your friend Maria, who is pregnant, has been feeling moody, anxious, and fearful. Describe three techniques that could help reduce her stress.

_____

_____

_____

_____

(Continued on next page)

Preparing for Birth

Section 5–2: Preparing for the Baby's Arrival

16. Describe how a woman pregnant with her second child might tell her three year old about the expected baby.

_____

_____

_____

_____

17. When choosing a new crib or accepting a used crib, what features of the crib should parents check?

_____

_____

_____

_____

_____

_____

18. Give three advantages of breast-feeding. _____

_____

_____

19. What are two possible reasons a mother may choose to bottle-feed? How does the cost of bottle-feeding compare to the cost of breast-feeding?

_____

_____

_____

_____

_____

20. What type of doctor specializes in treating children? _____

21. How can making a budget help expectant parents? _____

_____

_____

(Continued on next page)

22. What are *fixed expenses*? Give two examples. _____

_____

_____

23. What are *flexible expenses*? Give two examples. _____

_____

_____

24. Give three examples of expenses associated with pregnancy and childbirth. _____

_____

_____

_____

25. Where is the safest place for an infant in a car? _____

_____

_____

26. When deciding whether to work after a child is born, what factors should parents consider?

_____

_____

_____

_____

27. How does federal law provide for *maternity* and *paternity leave*? _____

_____

_____

_____

_____

Section 5–3: Childbirth Options

28. What is *prepared childbirth*? How does it benefit a pregnant woman? _____

_____

_____

_____

_____

(Continued on next page)

29. What is the difference between *labor* and *delivery*? _____

_____

_____

30. Give four examples of things expectant parents can learn from taking childbirth education classes.

_____

_____

_____

_____

_____

31. Describe the qualifications of each of the following health practitioners who deliver babies.

A. Obstetricians: _____

_____

B. Family doctors: _____

_____

C. Certified midwives: _____

_____

D. Certified nurse-midwives: _____

_____

32. Give two reasons why a couple might choose an *alternative birth center.* _____

_____

_____

_____

33. Why are hospitals generally the safest places to give birth? _____

_____

_____

_____

_____

_____

A Healthy Pregnancy

Planning a Healthy Diet

Directions: Your friend Talia is pregnant. She has asked your advice on nutrition. Complete the chart below to help Talia plan a healthy diet.

Food Category	Healthy Choices	Advice
Fruits	Oranges, bananas, dried apricots, peaches, orange juice	
Vegetables		Eat plenty of dark green leafy vegetables for folic acid to reduce risk of brain and spinal defects. Also eat orange vegetables, beans, and peas.
Milk		
Grains		
Meat & Beans		

(Continued on next page)

A Healthy Pregnancy   *Section 5–1 continued*

> **Directions:** Based on the information in your table on the previous page, plan a day's menu for Talia in the spaces below.

Breakfast:

Lunch:

Afternoon Snack:

Dinner:

Bedtime Snack:

The Developing Child: **Student Activity Manual**

Name _____ Date _____ Class _____

Preparing for the Baby's Arrival

Budgeting for a Baby

Directions: Budgeting for a new baby requires careful planning. Read the following description of a couple preparing for their first child. Then answer the questions that follow.

Jamal and Denise are expecting their first baby. Jamal is a branch manager at a local bank and earns $2,800 per month. Denise wants to stay home and care for the baby after the birth.

The couple rents a two-bedroom apartment for $750 per month. In addition, they pay an average of $60 per month for phone expenses and $180 a month for other utilities. They've figured out they also spend $60 per month on repairs and maintenance.

Denise and Jamal have some other significant expenses. They pay $200 every month on their car loan and have 22 months yet to pay. Gas and car maintenance average another $150 a month. Car and renters' insurance cost $1,800 per year. Some medical insurance coverage with Jamal's job, but they spend about $155 more per month on medical insurance premiums and health care. While they've stopped using credit cards, they are paying off their balance with $110 each month. They put $150 in a savings account monthly.

Denise takes an exercise class that cost $10 each week, Jamal golfs, which costs the same. They also spend about $20 a week on entertainment, such as movies, renting videos, or bowling. They spend about $60 a month on clothes and $15 a month for cleaning the clothes. Groceries run about $125 a week. Miscellaneous expenses are about $100 a month.

1. Use the information described above to complete the missing items in the following list. Assume that four weeks is a month.

Budget Category	Amount per Month	Budget Category	Amount per Month
Food		Utilities (average)	
Car/renters insurance		Telephone	
Medical		Auto loan payment	
Clothing and laundry		Car expenses	
Credit card payments		Home maintenance	
Recreation		Miscellaneous	
Housing		Savings	
		Total Monthly Expenses	

(Continued on next page)

Preparing for the Baby's Arrival

2. Which of the categories listed on the previous page are fixed expenses? _____

_____

_____

_____

3. Which of the categories listed above are flexible expenses? _____

_____

_____

_____

4. Which categories are likely to see higher expenses after the baby is born? List each category and explain why you think its cost will increase.

_____

_____

_____

_____

_____

_____

_____

5. What categories could they cut expenses to make room for these added costs? _____

_____

_____

_____

_____

_____

_____

_____

_____

Childbirth Options

Questions About Childbirth Options

Directions: Read each of the following situations. Then, in the spaces that follow, give your best advice to the person speaking.

1. "I want to have my baby delivered by a midwife. What qualifications do midwives have?" _____

    _____

    _____

    _____

    _____

2. "My husband and I moved here just three months ago, over a thousand miles away from our family and friends. I just found out that I'm pregnant. Although my doctor is someone suggested by a friend, I'm not sure she's the one for me. How soon do I need to make my decision, or is it already too late?"

    _____

    _____

    _____

3. "My husband is insisting that I have our baby in the hospital where he was born and with his family's doctor. I want to go to an alternative birth center near here. How can I change his mind?"

    _____

    _____

    _____

4. "My mother says I should use a certified nurse-midwife. Is that a good idea?" _____

    _____

    _____

5. "My husband thinks we should attend childbirth education classes. Childbirth is natural, right? Why do we need classes?"

    _____

    _____

    _____

    _____

(Continued on next page)

The Baby's Arrival

Study Guide

Directions: Answer the following questions as you read the chapter. They will help you focus on the main points. Later, you can use this guide to review and study the chapter information.

Section 6–1: Labor and Birth

1. What is happening when "lightening" occurs? _____
_____
_____

2. What is the "bloody show," and what does it mean for the pregnant woman? _____
_____
_____
_____

3. Explain what occurs when a woman's "water breaks." _____
_____
_____

4. What are *contractions*? What is their purpose? _____
_____
_____

5. What is the purpose of fetal monitoring during labor? _____
_____
_____

6. When is labor considered premature? What are the warning signs? _____
_____
_____
_____

(Continued on next page)

7. How can you distinguish false labor from real contractions? _____

_____

_____

_____

_____

8. Summarize the three stages of labor by completing the table below.

Stage of Labor	What Takes Place?	How Long Does It Last?
First		First child: Later children:
Second		First child: Later children:
Third		

9. What is a "breech presentation"? Why is it a complication? _____

_____

_____

10. How is the hormone "relaxin" related to dilation? _____

_____

_____

_____

11. What is an episiotomy, and why is it done? _____

_____

_____

12. What are *stem cells*, and why are they important? _____

_____

_____

_____

_____

(Continued on next page)

The Baby's Arrival

13. What is a *cesarean birth*? Why is this kind of delivery sometimes necessary? _____
_____
_____
_____
_____

14. What factors increase the chances of premature birth? _____
_____
_____
_____

15. Why does a premature baby usually need an *incubator*? _____
_____
_____
_____
_____

Section 6–2: The Newborn

16. What are *fontanels*? How do they affect the newborn's appearance? _____
_____
_____
_____
_____

17. Why does a newborn's head appear to be very large in proportion to the rest of the body?
_____
_____
_____
_____

18. What physical adjustments do newborns' bodies make to survive outside the uterus?
_____
_____
_____
_____
_____

(Continued on next page)

The Developing Child: **Student Activity Manual**

19. What is *lanugo*, and what happens to it? _____

_____

_____

20. When nurses give the newborn its first bath, what are they washing away? What is the purpose of this substance?

_____

_____

_____

21. What is the purpose of the *Apgar scale*? What five areas does it rate? _____

_____

_____

_____

22. Identify two other medical procedures that are performed shortly after birth and tell the purpose of each.

_____

_____

_____

_____

_____

23. What steps are taken to record a newborn's identity? _____

_____

_____

_____

Section 6–3: The Postnatal Period

24. What are some things a new mother can do to begin *bonding* with her newborn? _____

_____

_____

_____

25. How do bonding activities affect the baby's brain? _____

_____

_____

(Continued on next page)

The Baby's Arrival

26. What is *colostrum*? How does it help the baby? _____
_____
_____

27. What period of time is considered the *neonatal period*? _____
_____

28. A new mother is frightened. Her new baby's skin and eyes appear slightly yellow. What is this condition, and what causes it? Does it require treatment?
_____
_____
_____
_____

29. What do *lactation consultants* do? _____

30. Describe two benefits of *rooming-in*. _____
_____
_____
_____

31. What two legal forms should parents complete for their new baby? _____
_____
_____

32. Identify three physical problems typical of premature babies. _____
_____
_____

33. Summarize the physical needs of a new mother during the *postnatal period*. ____
_____
_____

34. Compare and contrast "baby blues" with *postpartum depression*. How are they similar? How are they different?
_____
_____
_____
_____
_____

Labor and Birth

Giving Advice About Labor

> **Directions:** Imagine that you are a nurse in the hospital's birthing center. You receive the following phone calls from pregnant women or their spouses. How would you respond to the calls? Write your responses on the spaces provided.

1. "Nurse, my wife is having contractions! I think we should get her to the hospital right away!"

   _____
   _____
   _____
   _____

2. "Nurse, I'm really worried. A gush of fluid just flowed out of me. Does that mean the baby is in danger? What should I do?"

   _____
   _____
   _____
   _____

3. "My contractions are five minutes apart. They've been holding steadily at about this cycle for more than an hour now. I've tried walking around, but the contractions continued. They're strong but not painful. Since I've already had two babies, I think I should go to the hospital soon—my last labor was very fast."

   _____
   _____
   _____
   _____

4. "Nurse, I'm having contractions eight minutes apart, and a little fluid is coming out. I've been pregnant only 35 weeks, so this is false labor, right?"

   _____
   _____

Name _____ Date _____ Class _____

The Newborn

What You Need to Know About Newborns

Directions: The list that follows shows topics from the notes of a doctor who was scheduled to speak to a class on "The Hospital's Role in Newborn Care." The doctor has been called away, and can't give his talk. Your job is to take his place, assembling important topics into an organized sequence. Some of the topics the doctor listed are not relevant to the subject of the talk. Cross those out before organizing your presentation. Then, using the textbook and any other sources, write out the major points you will include about each topic.

- Government funding for research on premature babies
- First hour after birth
- Apgar test and what it means
- Other tests after birth

- Cesarean births and when they're necessary
- Stages of labor
- Identifying the baby
- Newborn's appearance

_____

_____

_____

_____

_____

_____

_____

_____

_____

_____

_____

_____

_____

_____

_____

_____

_____

_____

_____

_____

_____

The Postnatal Period   **SECTION 6–3**

Meeting Baby's Needs

Directions: Recognizing and meeting a new baby's needs can be challenging. Read the following description of one couple's situation, and then answer the questions that follow.

Brittany and Kevin are excited about being first-time parents. Brittany is bottle-feeding their three-week-old son Joey. Brittany is sleeping only a few hours at a time because of Joey's feeding schedule. She feels exhausted. Kevin helps out when he can, but his work schedule is demanding. He doesn't get home until Joey's bedtime. Kevin just gives Joey a hug before Brittany cuddles him to sleep.

Money is tight, so they take Joey to a low-cost clinic for his regular check-ups. Kevin's mother gave Joey a mobile for his crib, but they can't afford other toys.

Both parents had a weight problem during childhood. When Joey began to gain weight, they decided to cut back on feedings. They wanted Joey to be able to keep a healthy weight throughout life.

1. What needs does Joey have at this age? _____

_____

_____

2. In what ways are Brittany and Kevin meeting Joey's needs? In what ways can they improve their care?

_____

_____

_____

_____

_____

_____

3. What can Kevin do in his limited time to bond more with Joey? _____

_____

_____

_____

4. How can Brittany and Kevin help Joey's intellectual development even if they can't afford many toys?

_____

_____

_____

_____

The Developing Child: **Student Activity Manual**

Name _____ Date _____ Class _____

Physical Development of Infants

Study Guide

> **Directions:** Answer the following questions as you read the chapter. They will help you focus on the main points. Later, you can use this guide to review and study the chapter information.

Section 7–1: Infant Growth and Development

1. Do the terms "growth" and "development" mean the same thing? Explain. _____
   _____
   _____
   _____

2. Give an example of each of the following patterns of development.
   A. Head to toe: _____
   _____
   _____

   B. Near to far: _____
   _____

   C. Simple to complex: _____
   _____
   _____

3. What are *developmental milestones*, and why are they useful? _____
   _____
   _____
   _____

4. Will inherited talents always emerge in children? Why or why not? _____
   _____
   _____
   _____

5. Why is proper nutrition essential for an infant? _____
   _____
   _____
   _____

(Continued on next page)

The Developing Child: **Student Activity Manual**

6. How does good health influence an infant's development? _____

_____

_____

_____

7. Is it the quantity or variety of experiences a child has that impacts brain development?

_____

8. What makes a place a *stimulating environment* for a baby? _____

_____

_____

9. Use the growth chart on page 214, to determine whether each of the following statements is True or False.

    A. At one year of age, boys are typically longer than girls. _____

    B. At birth, boys and girls typically weigh about the same. _____

    C. Between the ages of 3 months and 12 months, girls typically weigh less than boys. _____

10. Using your understanding of averages, explain when parents should become concerned if their baby is above or below average in weight according to growth charts.

_____

_____

_____

_____

11. Describe how the development of *depth perception* impacts a baby's interaction with the world.

_____

_____

12. Classify each of the following movements as a *reflex, gross motor skill,* or *fine motor skill.*

    A. Rolling over: _____

    B. Drinking from a cup: _____

    C. Sucking: _____

    D. Crawling: _____

    E. Grabbing a finger placed in the baby's hand: _____

    F. Picking up food with the thumb and forefinger: _____

13. At about what age do babies usually take their first steps alone? _____

14. Why is the development of *hand-eye coordination* important? _____

_____

_____

(Continued on next page)

Physical Development of Infants   *Chapter 7 continued*

Section 7–2: Infant Care Skills

15. What special precaution must be taken when picking up or holding a newborn? _____
_____
_____

16. What causes *shaken baby syndrome*? What are its possible consequences? _____
_____
_____
_____
_____

17. A month-old baby won't stop crying. The parent is starting to feel angry and is afraid of losing control. What would you recommend?
_____
_____
_____
_____

18. Why should you remove stuffed toys from the crib when putting the baby to bed? _____
_____

19. How should you position a baby in bed to help prevent sudden infant death syndrome (SIDS)?
_____

20. Ten minutes after Josh and Cheri put their baby Nathan to bed, he is still crying. Nathan is ten days old? What should they do?
_____
_____
_____

21. Give two examples of foods that usually work well as a baby's first solid foods. _____
_____

22. Why do experts discourage giving babies fruit juice during their first six months? _____
_____

(Continued on next page)

23. Describe three advantages of breast-feeding. _____
_____
_____
_____

24. What are two possible reasons for using formula? _____
_____
_____
_____

25. How much should an infant be allowed to eat? _____
_____
_____

26. When a baby begins to self-feed, some foods should be avoided because they may cause choking. Give three examples of such foods. _____
_____
_____

27. Why is it necessary to burp the baby during a feeding? _____
_____
_____
_____

28. What is *weaning*? About when are babies ready to wean? _____
_____
_____

29. When the baby is ready for solid foods, new foods should be introduced at least four days apart. Why?
_____
_____
_____

30. What condition could result if a baby does not receive enough of the right types of foods?
_____

31. About how warmly should you dress a baby compared to an adult? _____
_____

32. Give two characteristics you would look for when buying clothes for babies. _____
_____
_____
_____

(Continued on next page)

Section 7–3: Infant Health and Wellness

33. When babies reach the age of two or three months, about how often should you bathe them?

_____

_____

34. What are the symptoms of *cradle cap*? _____

_____

35. How can you treat *diaper rash*? _____

_____

_____

_____

36. Briefly summarize the steps involved in changing a diaper. _____

_____

_____

37. At about what age do babies begin *teething*? _____

38. Give three signs that a baby may be teething. _____

_____

_____

_____

39. How can you reduce a baby's risk of injury from falling? _____

_____

_____

40. How do *immunizations* work to protect against disease? _____

_____

_____

_____

_____

Name _____ Date _____ Class _____

Infant Growth and Development

Tracking Infant Development

Directions: For each motor skill described below, identify the *average age* at which the skill is first developed. Write the appropriate age from the box below in the blank in front of each skill description.

Ages		
1 month	5–6 months	9–10 months
2 months	7–8 months	11–12 months
3–4 months		

Months	Motor Skills
_____	1. Sits up steadily.
_____	2. Holds head up steadily.
_____	3. Turns head in direction of sounds.
_____	4. Lifts head when placed on stomach.
_____	5. May walk alone.
_____	6. Rolls from tummy to back.
_____	7. Puts objects in containers.
_____	8. Passes a block from one hand to the other.
_____	9. Watches the movement of objects close by.
_____	10. Picks up small objects using thumb and forefinger.
_____	11. Rolls over both ways.
_____	12. Puts objects into and takes them out of containers.
_____	13. Crawls well on hands and knees.
_____	14. Rocks on stomach while kicking legs and making swimming motions with arms.
_____	15. Stands with assistance.

16. Based on your responses, what is one of the first motor skills that infants acquire? _____

_____

Infant Care Skills

SECTION 7–2

Promoting Infant Health

Directions: Read the following descriptions of parents' care. If the action described promotes health, write **Yes** in the space to the left of the description. If the action does not promote health, write **No** in the space and explain why.

_____ **1.** Each night, Joni follows the same bedtime routine. She holds her son and rocks in a rocking chair while reading him a story. Then she places him in the crib on his stomach and pats his back gently.

_____

_____

_____

_____

_____ **2.** Mariana laughed at what her friend said. "No, I don't find breast-feeding to be embarrassing or difficult. It's easier than dealing with bottles. We're doing fine."

_____

_____

_____

_____ **3.** Josh was frustrated. His daughter wouldn't stop crying. The more he tried to calm her, the more tense her body felt in his arms. Shaking her, he shouted, "You've got to stop!"

_____

_____

_____

_____ **4.** After his baby had fed for a while, Miguel took the bottle away and put it on the table. "You can have more in a minute, baby," he said. "First, though, Daddy needs to burp you."

_____

_____

_____

_____

_____ **5.** Jonathan cradled his daughter close, supporting her head and body as he fed her a bottle of formula. She did not finish the entire bottle. Jonathan put the bottle in the refrigerator to give her in the next feeding.

_____

_____

_____

_____

_____ **6.** Brooke put her son into his crib at bedtime. "Here's your bottle, Connor. If you get hungry, you can have some." Then she put the nipple of the bottle into Connor's mouth.

_____

_____

_____

Name _____ Date _____ Class _____

Infant Health and Wellness

Keeping an Infant Safe and Well

Directions: Complete the chart by answering the questions in the spaces provided.

Bathing	Diapering	Safety
Until the navel heals, how should a baby be bathed?	About how many times each day does a very young baby need a diaper change?	Why is it important to keep all small objects off of floors?
When is it safe to begin bathing the baby in a full-size tub?	How can you recognize diaper rash?	How can you reduce a baby's risk of poisoning?
Beginning at age two to three months, about how often should babies have baths?	Which is more effective at keeping babies dry: cloth or disposable diapers?	Why should stuffed animals be kept out a baby's crib?
How should you test the temperature of a baby's bath water?	What should you do after removing a soiled diaper and before putting on a fresh diaper?	At what temperature should a water heater be set to avoid burning a baby?

Name _____ Date _____ Class _____

Emotional and Social Development of Infants

Study Guide

Directions: Answer the following questions as you read the chapter. They will help you focus on the main points. Later, you can use this guide to review and study the chapter information.

Section 8–1: Understanding Emotional Development of Infants

1. Distinguish between *emotional development* and *social development*. When do both begin? _____

_____

_____

_____

_____

2. How are emotional and social development related? _____

_____

3. What are the five basic emotions? _____

4. What is *attachment*? Why is it important to a baby? _____

_____

_____

_____

5. What do psychologist Harry Harlow's experiments with monkeys suggest about the importance of attachment.

_____

_____

_____

_____

6. Describe a situation that could lead to *failure to thrive*. How might this condition affect this person as an adult?

_____

_____

_____

_____

(Continued on next page)

7. Describe ways to build a sense of trust in a baby. _____

_____

_____

_____

_____

8. What is *temperament*? _____

_____

_____

9. Match each temperament trait to the correct description below.

Temperament Traits		
Perceptiveness	Adaptability	Sensitivity
Mood	Energy	First reaction
Intensity	Persistence	Regularity

A. Strength or weakness of emotional responses to events and to other people. _____

B. Determination to complete an action. _____

C. Strength of reaction to a person's own feelings. _____

D. Awareness of surroundings and tendency to be distracted by new things. _____

E. Ability to adjust to changes. _____

F. Tendency to follow set patterns in daily life. _____

G. Level of physical activity. _____

H. Degree of comfort with new situations. _____

I. Tendency to have a positive or negative outlook. _____

10. A crying baby doesn't seem to be hungry, in need of changing, hot or cold, or in need of burping. Describe three things you could try to comfort the baby.

_____

_____

_____

_____

11. Compare the symptoms of *colic* and *reflux*. How are they similar? How are they different?

_____

_____

_____

_____

_____

(Continued on next page)

The Developing Child: **Student Activity Manual**

Emotional and Social Development of Infants   ***Chapter 8 continued***

12. What precautions should be taken if a baby is given a pacifier? _____

_____

_____

_____

13. How does the emotional climate among the adults in the home affect the baby? _____

_____

_____

_____

Section 8–2: Understanding Social Development of Infants

14. A baby's eyes can follow moving objects at about what age? _____

_____

15. At about what age can babies distinguish between family members? _____

_____

16. What can a parent do to reduce *stranger anxiety* when introducing a baby to a new person?

_____

_____

_____

_____

17. How do babies learn social behaviors from caregivers? Give an example. _____

_____

_____

_____

18. Nine-month-old Andre grabbed the family cat by the tail and pulled on it. "No, Andre, that's not how we treat the cat," his mother said sharply. Then Andre's father said, "Look at the funny expression on the cat's face," and laughed. How might Andre respond to these messages?

_____

_____

_____

_____

(Continued on next page)

The Developing Child: **Student Activity Manual**

19. How are play and social development related? _____

_____

_____

_____

20. Describe a way that the caregiver can encourage an eight-month-old to crawl. _____

_____

_____

_____

21. What are the characteristics of a good *play environment*? _____

_____

_____

_____

22. A baby pours a cup of water on the floor and then splashes her hand in it repeatedly. Why is she doing this?

_____

_____

_____

23. How is exploration linked to play? _____

_____

Understanding Emotional Development of Infants

What Is Your Temperament?

Directions: Reread the description of temperament traits on pages 260-261 in the textbook. Then use the scale below to rate yourself in each area by circling the number that seems to match you best. When you finish, answer the questions that follow.

	Low		Average		High
Intensity	1	2	3	4	5
Persistence	1	2	3	4	5
Sensitivity	1	2	3	4	5
Perceptiveness	1	2	3	4	5
Adaptability	1	2	3	4	5
Regularity	1	2	3	4	5
Energy	1	2	3	4	5
First Reaction	Stays back 1	2	3	4	Dives in 5
Mood	Negative 1	2	3	4	Positive 5

1. Based on how you rated yourself, how would you describe your temperament?

_____

_____

_____

_____

2. Which two traits do you think are the most important for successful parenting? Why?

_____

_____

_____

_____

Understanding Social Development
of Infants

Milestones in Social Development

Directions: Read the descriptions of babies' behaviors below. From each description, identify the *average age* at which the behavior first appears. In the blank in front of the description, write the correct age from the box below.

Ages		
1 month	4–6 months	9–10 months
2–3 months	7–8 months	11–12 months

Months	Behaviors
_____	1. Shontel reached out to her mother and said "Mama."
_____	2. When Brandon's father left him alone, Brandon began to cry.
_____	3. Elena cooed and babbled happily in her playpen.
_____	4. When Ashley heard her grandmother's voice, she turned in that direction.
_____	5. David seemed fascinated with the word "no." He said it over and over.
_____	6. For the first time, Kareem began to smile and show excitement.
_____	7. Uncle Michael came to visit, but when Mia's mother tried to put her in his arms, Mia cried and clung to her mother.
_____	8. Alyssa enjoyed playing with other children.
_____	9. While drinking from his bottle, Jason maintained brief eye contact with his mother.
_____	10. Katie cried a lot, but when her father picked her up and spoke to her softly, she quieted down.
_____	11. When Matthew's sister took his toy away, Matthew began to cry.
_____	12. Camille enjoyed looking into a mirror and patting it with her hand.
_____	13. When his mother was out of the room, Marcus crawled around to look for her.
_____	14. Zach pointed vigorously toward the toy he wanted.
_____	15. Madison's mom knew what Madison needed from the sound of her cry.

Intellectual Development in Infants   **CHAPTER 9**

Study Guide

> **Directions:** Answer the following questions as you read the chapter. They will help you focus on the main points. Later, you can use this guide to review and study the chapter information.

Section 9–1: Early Brain Development

1. What are *neurons*? _____

2. What are *neural pathways*? What causes them to develop? _____
_____
_____
_____

3. Both a newborn and a six-month-old may kick their covers off if they feel warm. How is this response different for these two babies?
_____
_____

4. Newborns learn about the world through their senses. What part of the brain receives this sensory information?
_____

5. What part of the cerebrum allows more complex learning? _____

6. What role do *axons* and *dendrites* play in the brain? _____
_____

7. Explain the role of *neurotransmitters* in communicating between neurons. _____
_____
_____
_____

8. Explain how the brain becomes organized with neural pathways. _____
_____
_____

9. After stacking blocks repeatedly, a baby becomes skilled at stacking them quickly. How does the development of connections in the brain explain this skill?
_____
_____
_____

(Continued on next page)

The Developing Child: **Student Activity Manual**

10. What can a caregiver do to help the development of a baby's brain pathways? _____

_____

_____

_____

_____

11. What is *myelin*? How does its presence in the brain affect learning? _____

_____

_____

_____

_____

Section 9–2: Intellectual Development During the First Year

12. How is perception related to learning? _____

_____

_____

13. Give an example of each of the four intellectual abilities that babies develop in their first year.

A. Memory: _____

_____

_____

B. Associations: _____

_____

C. Cause and effect: _____

_____

D. Attention span: _____

_____

_____

_____

14. According to Piaget, how do children progress through the stages of intellectual development?

_____

_____

_____

_____

(Continued on next page)

Intellectual Development in Infants

15. Fill in the missing information with details about Piaget's four periods of intellectual development.

Period	Age	Characteristics
	Birth to 2 years	
	2 to 7 years	
		Can think logically but still learn best through experience.
Formal operations		

16. Keesha drops her toy and it rolls behind a chair. She realizes that the toy must be somewhere, even though she can't see it, so she crawls to look for it. What concept has Keesha learned?

_____

17. What type of thinking makes it possible for children to eventually learn to read? At about what age do children develop this capability?

_____

_____

_____

18. Why is it important to provide stimulation for an infant's senses during the first period of development that Piaget identified?

_____

_____

_____

_____

19. Give two examples of things a caregiver can do to build an infant's sense of security and trust.

_____

_____

_____

_____

20. What are concepts? _____

_____

_____

(Continued on next page)

21. Describe three stages that children ages one to three go through in beginning to learn words and learn *concepts.*

_____

_____

_____

_____

Section 9–3: Helping Infants Learn

22. How does responding to a child's cries help the child's intellectual abilities develop?

_____

_____

_____

_____

23. How can learning about average child development help parents and other caregivers encourage learning?

_____

_____

_____

_____

24. How does talking to infants benefit them? _____

_____

_____

_____

25. Why is *childproofing* the home better for intellectual development than keeping crawling or walking babies in playpens?

_____

_____

_____

_____

26. Name three ways that play benefits babies. _____

_____

_____

_____

(Continued on next page)

Name _____ Date _____ Class _____

Intellectual Development in Infants

Chapter 9 continued

27. Give an example of a toy that is good for a twelve-month-old but not for a four-month old. Explain why it is suitable for one age but not the other.

_____
_____
_____
_____
_____
_____

28. How do babies communicate before they can use words? _____
_____
_____

29. Why should caregivers avoid using baby talk? _____
_____
_____

30. Identify the average age range for each of the following speech milestones.
    A. Puts two words together: _____
    B. Voices excitement and displeasure: _____
    C. Talks about activities: _____
    D. Says one or two words: _____
    E. Tells stories: _____

Name _____ Date _____ Class _____

Early Brain Development

Understanding Brain Structure

Directions: The descriptions below explain some functions and characteristics of different parts of the brain. Write the name of the correct part of the brain in the space after its function. The same part of the brain may be used more than once. Then complete the diagram by writing the name of the brain part in the appropriate space.

```
        Parts of the Brain
  • Thalamus          • Brain stem
  • Spinal cord       • Cerebrum
  • Pituitary gland   • Cerebellum
```

1. Controls involuntary activities such as breathing. _____

2. Directs motor activities. _____

3. Controls the way emotions are expressed. _____

4. Coordinates the activities of the two sides of the body. _____

5. Secretes hormones that regulate growth. _____

6. Controls functions such as speech and memory. _____

7. Controls muscular coordination, balance, and posture. _____

8. Controls simple reflexes that do not involve the brain. _____

9. The cortex is the outer layer of this part of the brain. _____

10. Releases hormones that control metabolism and sexual development. _____

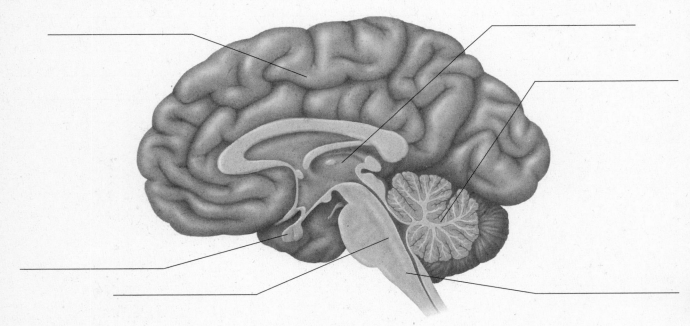

(Continued on next page)

Early Brain Development   *Section 9–1 continued*

Directions: Choose terms from the box below to label the parts of a neuron. Write the term in the appropriate place on the diagram. In the spaces below the diagram, briefly summarize the function of each part in transmitting information between neurons.

Parts of a Neuron
- Axon
- Cell body
- Dendrite
- Myelin
- Synapse

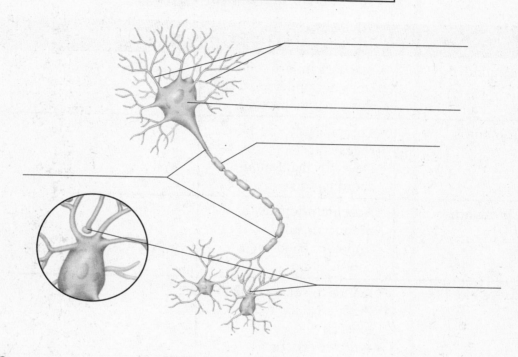

Functions

Dendrite: _____
_____
_____

Cell body: _____
_____

Axon: _____
_____

Myelin: _____
_____

Synapse: _____
_____
_____

Name _____ Date _____ Class _____

Intellectual Development

Applying Piaget's Work

> **Directions:** The chart below shows the stages and characteristics of intellectual development that Piaget placed in the sensorimotor period—the first of the periods he identified. In the right column, write examples of activities or objects that could be given infants at each stage in order to match its characteristics.

Piaget's Sensorimotor Period

Ages	Characteristics	Activities or Objects
Birth to one month	• Practices inborn reflexes. • Does not understand self as a separate person.	
One to four months	• Combines two or more reflexes. • Develops hand-mouth coordination.	
Four to eight months	• Acts intentionally to produce results. • Improves hand-eye coordination	
Eight to twelve months	• Begins to solve problems. • Finds partially hidden objects. • Imitates others.	
Twelve to eighteen months	• Finds hidden objects. • Explores and experiments. • Understands that objects exist independently.	
Eighteen to twenty-four months	• Solves problems by thinking through sequences. • Can think using symbols. • Begins imaginative thinking.	

The Developing Child: **Student Activity Manual**

Helping Infants Learn

Toy Evaluation

> **Directions:** Select a toy that might be appropriate for a child between seven and twelve months old. You may select a toy that you have seen in stores, catalogs, magazines, or around your home or the home of someone you know. Write the name of the toy and describe it below. If a picture is available, attach it to the page. Then answer the questions that follow.

Name of toy: _____

Description of toy: _____

_____

_____

_____

1. Why did you choose this toy? _____

_____

_____

2. What makes this toy safe or unsafe for this age range? _____

_____

_____

3. Would it be easy to keep clean? Explain. _____

_____

_____

_____

4. What materials are used in making this toy? _____

_____

_____

5. Is it durable and well constructed? Explain. _____

_____

_____

_____

(Continued on next page)

6. Check the information in the textbook about appropriate toys for children these ages. Would this toy really interest a child this age, or would it appeal more to older children or to the adults buying it? Explain.

_____

_____

_____

7. Does the toy encourage problem solving? Explain why or why not. _____

_____

_____

_____

8. What skills does the toy teach? _____

_____

_____

9. Would this toy stimulate a child's imagination or creativity? Why or why not? _____

_____

_____

10. Does the toy encourage interaction between children and adults? If so, how? _____

_____

_____

11. Can you think of any household objects that could substitute for this toy? Explain. _____

_____

_____

12. How many months do you think a child would enjoy this toy? Explain. _____

_____

_____

_____

Physical Development from One to Three

Study Guide

> **Directions:** Answer the following questions as you read the chapter. They will help you focus on the main points. Later, you can use this guide to review and study the chapter information.

Section 10–1: Growth and Development from One to Three

1. How old is a *toddler*? _____

2. Between what ages is a child referred to as a *preschooler*? _____
   _____

3. What factors, besides genes and heredity, influence growth and physical development? _____
   _____

4. How do height and weight gains change from age one to three? _____
   _____
   _____
   _____

5. Describe how body proportions change between ages two and three. _____
   _____
   _____

6. On average, about how many primary teeth emerge during a child's first year? Second year? Third year? How many primary teeth make up a full set?
   _____
   _____

7. At what age should a child start going to the dentist? Why? _____
   _____
   _____

8. Do all children reach developmental milestones at the same age? Why or why not?
   _____
   _____
   _____

9. How can learning about developmental milestones help caregivers plan activities? _____
   _____
   _____

(Continued on next page)

The Developing Child: **Student Activity Manual**

10. Give one example of a gross motor skill and one example a fine motor skill that is characteristic of each age group listed in the chart below.

Age	Gross Motor Skill	Fine Motor Skill
12 to 18 months		
18 to 24 months		
2 to 2½ years		
2½ to 3 years		

11. Which skill requires greater *dexterity*: walking steadily or turning on a faucet? Explain. _____
_____

12. What does the brain do in *sensory integration*? _____
_____

Section 10–2: Caring for Children from One to Three

13. Describe how nap and nighttime sleep patterns change between ages one and two. _____
_____
_____

14. How do *night terrors* differ from nightmares? Which is more serious? _____
_____
_____
_____

15. Compare the self-feeding abilities of one-, two-, and three-year-olds. _____
_____
_____
_____
_____
_____

(Continued on next page)

16. Should a growing two-year-old drink a full cup of milk or an entire apple or banana at one time? Why or why not?

_____

_____

_____

17. Give examples of each of the following ways to make meals appealing to children.

   A. Color: _____

_____

   B. Texture: _____

_____

   C. Shape: _____

_____

   D. Temperature: _____

_____

   E. Ease of eating: _____

_____

18. Give two tips for parents who are trying to teach their child good eating habits. _____

_____

_____

_____

_____

_____

19. List three basic *hygiene* skills that children can learn between the ages of one and three. _____

_____

_____

_____

20. Should toddlers be expected to brush their own teeth? Explain. _____

_____

_____

21. What are signs that a child is physically and emotionally ready for toilet teaching? _____

_____

_____

(Continued on next page)

22. At about what age are children physically able to control their *sphincter muscles*? _____

23. What are advantages and disadvantages of *synthetic fibers* for children's clothing? _____

_____

_____

_____

24. What does the term *flame-resistant* mean? Are all children's clothes required to be flame-resistant?

_____

_____

_____

25. How does a vaccine work to protect children from a disease? _____

_____

_____

_____

_____

26. Why can peeling paint be a health hazard for children? _____

_____

_____

_____

27. For each hazard below, give an example of how to reduce the risk for young children.

A. Choking: _____

_____

B. Unsafe toys: _____

_____

C. Poisoning: _____

_____

D. Burns: _____

_____

E. Traffic accidents: _____

_____

F. Sunburn: _____

_____

G. Pets: _____

_____

Growth and Development
from One to Three

Promoting Motor Skill Development

Directions: Motor skill development is a primary goal for one-, two-, and three-year-olds. The chart on page 315 in the text identifies fine and gross motor skills typically mastered during specific age spans. Similar lists are available on the Internet. Choose two of the age groups listed on the chart. For each age span, plan five developmentally appropriate activities that would aid development of specific motor skills. Categorize each skill as a fine motor or gross motor skill.

Age span 1: _____

Activity: Description:	Skill developed: Skill category:
Activity: Description:	Skill developed: Skill category:
Activity: Description:	Skill developed: Skill category:
Activity: Description:	Skill developed: Skill category:
Activity: Description:	Skill developed: Skill category:

(Continued on next page)

Age span 2:_____

Activity: Description:	Skill developed: Skill category:
Activity: Description:	Skill developed: Skill category:
Activity: Description:	Skill developed: Skill category:
Activity: Description:	Skill developed: Skill category:
Activity: Description:	Skill developed: Skill category:

Caring for Children from One to Three

Planning Meals for Young Children

Directions: Listed below are four menus for young children. Using information from Section 10-2, evaluate the meals to identify ways they could be improved. In the spaces below the menus, list at least two problems you see or suggestions you can make to improve the menus. Then complete the rest of the activity.

Menu A
Fried hamburger on a bun
French fries
Fried apple pies
Milk

Menu B
Meat loaf
Mashed potatoes
Applesauce
Grits
Vanilla pudding
Milk

Menu C
Meatballs
Green beans
Brussels sprouts
Dinner rolls
Dip of lime sherbet
Milk

Menu D
Baked trout
Baked potato
Stuffed acorn squash
Garlic bread
Milk

Evaluation

1. Menu A: _____

_____

_____

2. Menu B: _____

_____

_____

3. Menu C: _____

_____

_____

4. Menu D: _____

_____

_____

(Continued on next page)

5. How would you change two of these menus to make them more suitable for a child one to three years old? Make your new menus by crossing out and adding to the menus on the previous page. Bear in mind that you can change the type of food, the method of cooking, or the way of serving the food. In the lines below, explain why you made the changes.

_____

_____

_____

_____

_____

_____

_____

6. In the space below, plan a dinner menu for a three-year old. Specify serving amounts. Then evaluate the menu by circling either "Yes" or "No" to the left of the questions that follow.

Food   **Serving Size**

_____   _____

_____   _____

_____   _____

_____   _____

_____   _____

Yes   No   **A.** Are all food groups from Figure 10-9, page 326, represented?

Yes   No   **B.** Are the amounts appropriate for a three-year-old?

Yes   No   **C.** Does the meal contain a variety of colors?

Yes   No   **D.** Are the food textures varied?

Yes   No   **E.** Are the food shapes varied?

Yes   No   **F.** Can the foods be eaten easily by a three-year-old?

Yes   No   **G.** Does the menu avoid having too many strong flavors that a child
               might not like?

Name _____ Date _____ Class _____

Emotional and Social Development
from One to Three

Study Guide

> **Directions:** Answer the following questions as you read the chapter. They will help you focus on the main points. Later, you can use this guide to review and study the chapter information.

Section 11–1: Emotional Development from One to Three

1. Why are most children *self-centered* at eighteen months? _____
   _____

2. Identify and describe two causes for toddlers' *negativism*. _____
   _____
   _____
   _____
   _____

3. When are *temper tantrums* likely to start? At what age do they usually stop? _____
   _____

4. Identify which ages—eighteen months, two years, two and one-half years, and three years—are generally calmer and which generally have more frustrations.
   A. Calmer: _____
   B. More frustrations: _____

5. How do an eighteen-month-old and a three-year-old each typically express anger?
   _____
   _____
   _____

6. What are *phobias*? _____
7. What is *separation anxiety*? _____
   _____

8. Describe three ways that caregivers can help toddlers deal with their fears. _____
   _____
   _____
   _____
   _____
   _____

(Continued on next page)

9. Describe three things a parent can do to reduce *sibling rivalry*. _____

_____

_____

_____

_____

10. What is a sign that toddlers are developing *empathy*? _____

_____

11. What differences cause each child to develop emotionally in a unique way? _____

_____

_____

12. How do children form their *self-concept*? _____

_____

_____

_____

13. Why is it so important for toddlers to have a positive relationship with parents and siblings?

_____

_____

14. Describe at least two signs a child has a healthy relationship with a parent. _____

_____

_____

_____

_____

15. Identify the two cycles that make up sleep. Which cycle is a deep sleep? In which cycle do dreams occur?

_____

_____

16. What are two signs that a child may be *sleep-deprived*? Why is the condition more apparent after children start school?

_____

_____

_____

_____

_____

(Continued on next page)

Emotional and Social Development
from One to Three

Section 11–2: Social Development from One to Three

17. What is *socialization*? _____

_____

_____

_____

18. What is the difference between *parallel play* and *cooperative play*? Which comes first?

_____

_____

_____

_____

_____

19. How concerned with helping and pleasing others are children of the following ages? Describe how they demonstrate their level of concern.

   A. Two: _____

_____

_____

   B. Two and one-half: _____

_____

_____

   C. Three: _____

_____

_____

   D. Three and one-half: _____

_____

_____

20. What is a drawback to children spending almost all of their time with adults? _____

_____

_____

_____

_____

_____

_____

(Continued on next page)

21. At a child care center, two three-year-olds get into an argument. How should you respond? Why?

22. Jason is concerned about his three-year-old's unusual behavior. David has an imaginary friend that he talks to a lot. Jason is embarrassed and wants to put an end to it. What advice would you give Jason?

23. How does a parent's guidance help a child learn *self-discipline*?

24. When fourteen-month-old Kayla began running after the family dog, her mother said, "Kayla, look out the window at the little bunny." What method of guidance was she using? If Kayla were age two or older, what might her mother do to keep Kayla from hurting the dog?

25. Why is consistency important when setting limits?

(Continued on next page)

Name _____ Date _____ Class _____

Emotional and Social Development
from One to Three

Chapter 11 continued

26. What is *autonomy*? Give an example of how parents can encourage their child's autonomy in eating, dressing, hygiene, or household tasks.

_____

_____

_____

27. Describe three ways that caregivers can promote sharing among toddlers. _____

_____

_____

_____

_____

_____

_____

28. What kinds of aggressive behaviors do some two- and three-year-olds display? Is ignoring the misbehavior one acceptable course of action? Explain.

_____

_____

_____

_____

_____

Name _____ Date _____ Class _____

*Emotional Development
from One to Three*

Parenting Q & A

Directions: Read the following e-mail messages sent to Help for Parents' online question site. Take the role of the site's expert and write a response to each message. Write your responses in the spaces provided.

1. Help! Our three-year-old daughter has always seemed happy, but recently she started sucking her thumb again. She even wet her pants a couple times in the past week, something that hasn't happened for more than a year. What could be wrong? What should we do?

   _____

   _____

   _____

   _____

   _____

   _____

   _____

2. My two-year-old cries every time I drop him off at the child care center. The caregivers tell me that he's fine during the day, but it just breaks my heart to hear him cry. What should I do?

   _____

   _____

   _____

   _____

   _____

   _____

   _____

3. We're expecting our second baby in four months. What should we say to our three-year-old daughter?

   _____

   _____

   _____

   _____

   _____

   _____

(Continued on next page)

Emotional Development from One to Three

4. My two-year old has a temper tantrum almost every time we go to the supermarket. It's gotten to the point where I dread having to go to the store. How can I break him of this habit?

_____

_____

_____

_____

5. Ever since Brenna turned two, she says "no" to absolutely everything. When we ask if she's hungry, or ready to go someplace, or ready for bed—it doesn't matter what the question is. She always says "no"! How can we stop her?

_____

_____

_____

_____

6. Nguyen and I used to take a walk every afternoon, but, ever since a neighbor got a big dog, he doesn't want to go. The dog barked at him the first day, and he's been afraid to get near it ever since. How can I get him to enjoy his walks again?

_____

_____

_____

_____

7. My twins are two and one-half. They seem to disrupt family activities all the time. When I praise Kara for her block construction, Jimmy starts singing loudly nearby. When I admire Jimmy's coloring, Kara pushes her toy train across the page. What can I do?

_____

_____

_____

_____

Name _____ Date _____ Class _____

Social Development from One to Three

Analyzing Children's Behavior

Directions: Jake has been working as a volunteer at a local child care center. Each day when he's done, he talks to Kathleen Wallach, one of the center's teachers, about what he's seen that day. Read his questions from one day and then, in the spaces provided, write the answers you think Mrs. Wallach would give.

1. Shayna, who is two and one-half, sat for a long time just watching a boy about the same age play with blocks. Is there something wrong with her that she's not joining in?

   _____

   _____

   _____

   _____

2. Joe was talking about somebody named Justin. But there isn't anybody in the center or his family with that name. One of the other staff members said that this was Joe's imaginary friend. Is it okay for him to have an imaginary friend?

   _____

   _____

   _____

   _____

3. One time when two girls were fighting over who would play with the fire truck, you stepped in right away. They were about eighteen months old. Why didn't you let them work it out for themselves? Isn't it better for them to learn to solve their own problems?

   _____

   _____

   _____

   _____

4. You seemed to make a special point of praising that really quiet girl, Alexis. You told her how much you like her finger painting, how much she helped in handing out snacks, and how well she sang during the music time. Why make such a big fuss over her, when there are lots of other kids who do more or better than she does?

   _____

   _____

   _____

   _____

Intellectual Development
from One to Three

Study Guide

Directions: Answer the following questions as you read the chapter. They will help you focus on the main points. Later, you can use this guide to review and study the chapter information.

Section 12–1: Brain Development from One to Three

1. How has *neuroscience* benefited parents and other caregivers? _____
_____
_____
_____

2. What is *intelligence*. _____
_____
_____
_____

3. What roles do heredity and environment play in intelligence? _____
_____
_____
_____

4. What are the features of a stimulating environment that promotes intellectual development?
_____
_____
_____

5. Give examples of the four methods of learning, other than those used in the textbook.

   A. *Incidental learning*: _____
   _____
   _____
   _____

   B. *Trial and error learning:* _____
   _____
   _____
   _____

(Continued on next page)

C. *Imitation:* _____

_____

_____

_____

D. *Directed learning:* _____

_____

_____

6. What are concepts? Give three examples of concepts that young children learn. _____

_____

_____

7. Why do toddlers have difficulty concentrating on one thing at a time? _____

_____

_____

_____

8. Why is the ability to remember such an important key to learning? _____

_____

_____

9. How can parents help improve their child's perception? _____

_____

_____

10. Compare the problem-solving strategy of a fourteen-month-old to that of a three-year-old.

_____

_____

_____

11. Why is it important to respect a child's imagination? Should parents always point out what is real and what's not?

_____

_____

_____

_____

(Continued on next page)

12. How does *creativity* relate to imagination? _____

_____

_____

13. How might keeping a child in a playpen discourage curiosity? How might curiosity be mistaken for misbehavior?

_____

_____

_____

_____

Section 12–2: Encouraging Learning from One to Three

14. What is the meaning of "readiness for learning"? _____

_____

_____

15. How can a routine of reading to children younger than age three contribute to *reading readiness*?

_____

_____

_____

_____

_____

16. How can caregivers promote *math readiness* in young children? _____

_____

_____

_____

17. Three-year-old Terrell is having trouble closing a cabinet door because toys are sticking over the edge of the shelf. How should his father respond? Why?

_____

_____

_____

_____

_____

18. Scott's mom said "Grandpa's birthday card won't fit in this envelope. Let's see if we have a bigger envelope. Or we can fold the card if we have to." How was she modeling problem solving for Scott?

_____

_____

_____

(Continued on next page)

19. Identify three common safety hazards related to toys. _____

_____

_____

20. In addition to safety, identify six characteristics of appropriate toys. _____

_____

_____

_____

21. Give an example of a toy that is appropriate for each of the following age groups. Then give a developmental reason why the toy is appropriate.

    A. One to two years: _____

_____

    B. Two to three years: _____

_____

    C. Three to four years: _____

22. Why might children of two and a half use a word like "tooths"? _____

_____

_____

_____

23. What kinds of problems might a *speech-language pathologist* identify as the source of a child's speech difficulties?

_____

_____

24. How is difficulty with *articulation* different from *stuttering*? How are they similar?

_____

_____

_____

_____

_____

Brain Development from One to Three **SECTION 12–1**

A Young Child's Mind

Directions: Intellectual activity includes the seven components listed below. Referring to Chapter 12 of your textbook, explain and give an example of how each part relates to the thinking of a child ages one to three. Write as though you were explaining the topic to a friend or classmate.

1. **ATTENTION is** _____
_____

Example: _____
_____

2. **MEMORY is** _____
_____

Example: _____
_____

3. **PERCEPTION is** _____
_____

Example: _____
_____

4. **REASONING is** _____
_____

Example: _____
_____

5. **IMAGINATION is** _____
_____

Example: _____
_____

6. **CREATIVITY is** _____
_____

Example: _____
_____

7. **CURIOSITY is** _____
_____

Example: _____
_____

*Encouraging Learning
from One to Three*

SECTION 12–2

Writing About Children

> **Directions:** You are the editor of a magazine for parents. Your staff has given you several ideas for articles, which are listed below. Cross out any ideas that you think are poor ones and, in the spaces below, explain why. For the ideas that you think are good, write down the main points that the article should cover.

1. "Teach Your Two-Year-Old to Read" _____
   _____
   _____

2. "Parents as Teachers" _____
   _____
   _____
   _____

3. "The Year's Best Toys" _____
   _____
   _____
   _____

4. "How to Keep Toddlers from Interrupting" _____
   _____
   _____

5. "How to Talk to Your Child" _____
   _____
   _____
   _____

6. "Speech Problems—What You Can Do To Help Your Child" _____
   _____
   _____
   _____

Name _____ Date _____ Class _____

Physical Development
from Four to Six

Study Guide

Directions: Answer the following questions as you read the chapter. They will help you focus on the main points. Later, you can use this guide to review and study the chapter information.

Section 13–1: Growth and Development from Four to Six

1. How does the physical growth rate of children ages four to six compare to that of children ages one to three?

   _____

   _____

2. About how much height and weight do children gain per year from ages four to six?

   _____

   _____

3. Describe three ways a child's body shape and posture change from age four through age six.

   _____

   _____

   _____

   _____

   _____

4. Which *permanent teeth* appear first? What is their role in the arrangement of teeth in the mouth?

   _____

   _____

   _____

   _____

5. In what order are primary teeth lost? _____

   _____

   _____

(Continued on next page)

Physical Development from Four to Six

6. Five-year-old Tyler sucks his thumb a lot. His parents are concerned. What should they do and why?

_____

_____

_____

_____

_____

7. For each skill listed in the chart below, indicate whether it is a fine or gross motor skill. Identify the age—four, five, or six—when a child typically learns it.

Motor Skill	Fine or Gross?	Approximate Age
Writes entire words		
Skips, alternating feet		
Walks backward easily		
Cuts on line with scissors		
Buttons clothing		
Throws ball overhand		
Hops on one foot		
Draws a person with head, body, arms, and legs		
Dresses and undresses self		
Jumps rope		
Uses spoon and fork, but also uses fingers for some foods		

8. When are most children able to tie their shoes? _____

9. What are *ambidextrous* children able to do? _____

_____

Section 13–2: Caring for Children from Four to Six

10. Some children in this age group require more food than others. What factors account for this difference?

_____

_____

11. How often should children ages four to six eat? _____

_____

(Continued on next page)

12. "I hate peas," declared six-year-old Alexis. "If you eat all your peas, you can stay up an extra half-hour tonight," her mother responded. Is the mother's response likely to encourage good eating habits? Explain.

_____

_____

_____

13. How can parents model good eating habits? _____

_____

14. How can television viewing negatively influence a child's nutrition and physical health?

_____

_____

_____

15. Name three ways that children can be involved in obtaining and preparing food. _____

_____

_____

16. Why is it important the foods included in packed lunches are appealing, as well as nutritious?

_____

_____

_____

17. Why are convenience foods and foods from fast-food restaurants often poor nutritional choices?

_____

_____

18. What are three ways that poor nutrition can affect children's health and development?

_____

_____

_____

19. If a four- to six-year-old appears overweight, who can help them determine if there is a problem? Who can help with meal planning if there is one?

_____

_____

_____

(Continued on next page)

20. When a child consumes more calories than the body uses through physical activity, what happens to the extra calories?

_____

_____

21. When parents are trying to help their children be physically active, why is it important to choose activities that are age appropriate?

_____

_____

_____

22. What are two techniques that can be used to encourage four- to six-year-olds to bathe regularly?

_____

_____

_____

_____

23. At about what age are children able to handle a toothbrush well enough to brush without help?

_____

24. Why is it important for children to use a toothpaste that contains *fluoride?* _____

_____

_____

25. Cassandra never fussed about her clothing, but since her sixth birthday, she has refused to wear certain outfits. What might have caused this change?

_____

_____

_____

_____

26. At bedtime, six-year-old Garrett throws his clothes on the floor of his room. His mother puts them in the laundry hamper because it seems easier than constantly reminding Garrett to do it. Evaluate this mother's response to this problem.

_____

_____

_____

_____

_____

27. How much sleep do most four- to six-year-olds need each night? _____

_____

(Continued on next page)

Physical Development from Four to Six

28. How do they typically react to bedtime? _____

_____

_____

29. Identify four ways that parents should respond to bed wetting. _____

_____

_____

_____

_____

30. Beth's son Luis just turned four. When they arrive at his friend's birthday party at a recreation center, she makes sure he knows where the bathroom is. What else could Beth do to prevent a toileting accident?

_____

_____

_____

Growth and Development
From Four to Six

SECTION 13–1

Describing Growth and Development

Directions: Dr. Janna Pavlev, a pediatrician and author, is giving an illustrated lecture to parents about the growth and development of preschoolers. You are Dr. Pavlev's assistant. Listed below are descriptions of some of the PowerPoint® slides that Dr. Pavlev will show during her talk. In the lines below each description, write some notes that Dr. Pavlev can use as the basis for her talk.

1. Slide: A group of preschoolers standing together in class photo. Children are of different heights and weights.

   _____

   _____

   _____

   _____

2. Slide: Six-year-old boy standing next to two-year-old boy at backyard pool; both are in swimsuits so body shapes are evident.

   _____

   _____

   _____

   _____

3. Slide: Six-year-old girl smiling at camera missing two lower front teeth. _____

   _____

   _____

   _____

   _____

4. Slide: Children aged four to six running in park or playground. _____

   _____

   _____

   _____

   _____

   _____

Caring for Children from Four to Six

Using Nutrition Labels

Directions: When selecting a cereal, reading the fine print can help because all packaged foods are required by law to have a panel listing nutrition facts. Each contains information about serving size, calories, fat content, nutrients, and vitamins. One column shows the "% daily value." That figure tells how much of an adult's dietary needs are met by one serving of the product. In Cereal A below, for example, one serving provides 25% of the daily need for vitamin C. Study both labels and answer the questions that follow.

1. How big is a serving?

   Cereal A _____   Cereal B _____

2. What size serving would you estimate a four- to six-year-old might eat?

   _____

3. How many servings are in a box?

   Cereal A _____   Cereal B _____

4. How many calories are in each serving, both plain and with milk?

   Cereal A plain _____   Cereal B plain _____

   Cereal A with milk _____   Cereal B with milk _____

5. What are the four main ingredients (the first four listed) in each cereal?

   Cereal A _____

   _____

   Cereal B _____

   _____

   _____

6. Which cereal contains more fiber? _____

7. Which cereal provides more vitamin A? More iron?

   Vitamin A _____

   Iron _____

8. Does the vitamin C come from the cereal itself or from the milk?

   _____

9. In general, what characteristics do cereals advertised to appeal to children have?

   _____

   _____

Cereal A

Nutrition Facts
Serving Size   3/4 Cup (31g/1.1 oz)
Servings per Container   18

Amount Per Serving	Cereal	Cereal with ½ Cup Vitamins A & D Skim Milk
Calories	120	160
Fat Calories	0	0

	% Daily Value**	
Total Fat 0g*	0%	0%
Saturated Fat 0g	0%	0%
Polyunsaturated Fat 0g		
Monounsaturated Fat 0g		
Cholesterol 0mg	0%	0%
Sodium 210mg	9%	11%
Potassium 20mg	1%	6%
Total Carbohydrate 28g	9%	11%
Dietary Fiber 0g	0%	0%
Sugars 13g		
Other Carbohydrate 15g		
Protein 1g		

Vitamin A	15%	20%
Vitamin C	25%	25%
Calcium	0%	15%
Iron	10%	10%
Vitamin D	10%	25%
Thiamin	25%	30%
Riboflavin	25%	35%
Niacin	25%	25%
Vitamin B6	25%	25%
Folic Acid	25%	25%

*Amount in cereal. One half cup skim milk contributes an additional 40 calories, 65mg sodium, 6g total carbohydrate (6g sugars), and 4g protein.
**Percent Daily Values are based on a 2,000 calorie diet. Your daily values may be higher or lower depending on your calorie needs:

	Calories	2,000	2,500
Total Fat	Less than	65g	80g
Sat. Fat	Less than	20g	25g
Cholesterol	Less than	300mg	300mg
Sodium	Less than	2,400mg	2,400mg
Potassium		3,500mg	3,500mg
Total Carbohydrate		300mg	375g
Dietary Fiber		25g	30g

Calories per gram:
Fat 9 • Carbohydrate 4 • Protein 4

Ingredients: Corn, sugar, salt, malt flavoring, corn syrup.
Vitamins and Iron: ascorbic acid, (vitamin C), niacinamide, iron, pyridoxine hydrochloride (vitamin B6) riboflavin (vitamin B2), vitamin A palmitate (protected with BHT), thiamin hydrochloride (vitamin B1), folic acid, and vitamin D.

(Continued on next page)

The Developing Child: **Student Activity Manual**

10. If a child liked to eat dry cereal as a snack, which column would you look at for nutrition information? Why is more nutritious to eat cereal with milk?

_____

_____

_____

11. Some sweetened cereals contain 6g of sugar per serving. A serving of unsweetened cereal may contain about 3g of sugar. How much sugar does Cereal A contain? Cereal B? Would you classify them as sugary cereals?

Cereal A: _____   Cereal B: _____

_____

12. If these cereals were available as packaged breakfast bars, predict ways in which the nutrition information might change.

_____

_____

_____

_____

13. How might parents add even more nutrition to their five-year-old's morning cereal?

_____

_____

14. Would you serve either cereal to a child aged four to six? Why or why not?

_____

_____

_____

_____

_____

_____

Cereal B

Nutrition Facts
Serving Size ¾ Cup (30g)
Servings per Container 14

Amount Per Serving	Cereal	With ½ Cup Skim Milk
Calories	120	160
Calories from Fat	25	25

	% Daily Value**	
Total Fat 2.5g*	4%	4%
Saturated Fat 0g	0%	3%
Cholesterol 0mg	0%	1%
Sodium 180mg	8%	10%
Potassium 70mg	2%	8%
Total Carbohydrate 24g	8%	10%
Dietary Fiber 1g	6%	6%
Sugars 12g		
Other Carbohydrate 11g		
Protein 2g		
Vitamin A	25%	30%
Vitamin C	25%	25%
Calcium	4%	15%
Iron	25%	25%
Vitamin D	10%	25%
Thiamin	25%	30%
Riboflavin	25%	35%
Niacin	25%	25%
Vitamin B$_6$	25%	25%
Folic Acid	25%	25%
Phosphorus	6%	20%
Magnesium	4%	8%
Zinc	2%	6%
Copper	2%	2%

*Amount in cereal. A serving of cereal plus milk provides 0.5g saturated fat, <5mg cholesterol, 240mg sodium, 270mg potassium, 30g carbohydrate (18g sugar) and 6g protein.
**Percent Daily Values are based on a 2,000 calorie diet. Your daily values may be higher or lower depending on your calorie needs:

	Calories	2,000	2,500
Total Fat	Less than	65g	80g
Sat. Fat	Less than	20g	25g
Cholesterol	Less than	300mg	300mg
Sodium	Less than	2,400mg	2,400mg
Potassium		3,500mg	3,500mg
Total Carbohydrate		300mg	375g
Dietary Fiber		25g	30g

Calories per gram: Fat 9 • Carbohydrate 4 • Protein 4

INGREDIENTS: WHOLE OAT FLOUR (INCLUDES THE OAT BRAN), SUGAR, CORN SYRUP, DRIED APPLE PIECES, PARTIALLY HYDROGENATED SOYBEAN OIL, WHEAT STARCH, SALT, CINNAMON, CALCIUM CARBONATE, TRISODIUM PHOSPATE, COLOR AND FRESHNESS PRESERVED BY SODIUM SULFITE, SULFUR DIOXIDE AND BHT.
VITAMINS AND MINERALS: VITAMIN C (SODIUM ASCORBATE), A B VITAMIN (NIACIN), IRON (A MINERAL NUTRIENT), VITAMIN A (PALMITATE), VITAMIN B$_6$ (PYRIDOXINE HYDROCHLORIDE), VITAMIN B$_2$ (RIBOFLAVIN), VITAMIN B$_1$ (THIAMIN MONONITRATE), A B VITAMIN (FOLIC ACID) AND VITAMIN D.

*Emotional and Social Development
from Four to Six*

Study Guide

> **Directions.** Answer the following questions as you read the chapter. They will help you focus on the main points. Later, you can use this guide to review and study the chapter information.

Section 14–1: Emotional Development from Four to Six

1. What new challenges do children ages four to six face? _____

_____

_____

_____

_____

_____

2. Briefly describe the emotional characteristics of children of the following ages.

   A. Age four: _____

_____

_____

_____

_____

   B. Age five: _____

_____

_____

_____

   C. Age six: _____

_____

_____

_____

_____

_____

3. A four-year-old's active imagination can lead to fears. Why? _____

_____

_____

_____

_____

(Continued on next page)

The Developing Child: **Student Activity Manual**

4. What is *self-confidence*? What is initiative? How are they related? _____

_____

_____

_____

5. What characteristics might indicate that a child may have Attention Deficit Hyperactivity Disorder (ADHD)?

_____

_____

6. How do four- to six-year-olds differ from toddlers in the ways they express anger? _____

_____

_____

_____

7. Four-year-old Daniel doesn't want to sleep alone in his bedroom because he believes there is a ghost in his closet. How would you respond? _____

_____

_____

_____

8. How can parents and other caregivers help children work through jealous feelings? What responses should they avoid?

_____

_____

_____

9. Name at least four possible signs of stress or *tension* in preschoolers and kindergartners.

_____

_____

_____

10. Describe two techniques for discovering the cause of the stress. _____

_____

_____

_____

(Continued on next page)

Emotional and Social Development　　　　　　　　*Chapter 14 continued*
from Four to Six

11. When a child is showing symptoms of stress, should parents ease up on rules to reduce the stress? Why or why not?

_____

_____

_____

12. Name three ways to help preschoolers develop self-confidence. _____

_____

_____

_____

_____

_____

_____

Section 14–2: Social and Moral Development from Four to Six

13. Who are a preschooler's *peers*? Compare four-year-olds to toddlers in the way they relate to their peers during play.

_____

_____

_____

_____

_____

14. Use what you know about the general patterns of social development in four- to six-year-olds to identify the approximate age of the child in each description below.

   A. Erik and his neighbor rarely quarrel, and they no longer snatch each other's toys.

   _____

   B. Kaitlyn wants to spend even more time with her best friend than she did last year, but their parents are frustrated because they seem to bicker a lot.

   _____

   C. Shareef took his mother by the hand and brought him to the room where he was building interlocking blocks. "Look at my house!" Shareef said proudly.

   _____

   D. Megan begged to join a soccer team, but she paid little attention during practice and at the games.

   _____

   E. Connor told Kenny, "You know, Jackson still watches baby shows on television," and Kenny laughed]

   _____

(Continued on next page)

　　　The Developing Child: **Student Activity Manual**

15. Chase and Austin, both six, are playing with a plastic bat and a whiffle ball. Describe a situation that might result in *aggressive behavior* between them. As a counselor at a day camp, how would you help them resolve the problem?

_____

_____

_____

_____

16. Summarize two possible benefits and two possible drawbacks of *competition* as it pertains to children's development.

_____

_____

_____

_____

_____

_____

17. How can *competitive* team sports help develop cooperation? _____

_____

_____

18. In order for their child to be well-rounded, is it necessary for parents to sign their kindergartner up for a sports team?

_____

_____

_____

19. Summarize the changes in relationships with family members from ages four to six.

_____

_____

_____

_____

20. What is *moral development*? _____

_____

_____

(Continued on next page)

Emotional and Social Development
from Four to Six

21. What change in moral development takes place in the preschool years? How might this change affect how parents instruct preschoolers?

_____

_____

_____

_____

22. Working with a group of children, Lisa saw four-year-old Marissa hit Autumn in the play kitchen. Immediately Lisa told Marissa, "We do *not* hit others. Hitting hurts. You're never going to have any friends if you act like that." Then she made a point of ignoring Marissa the rest of the afternoon. What did Lisa do right? What did she do wrong?

_____

_____

_____

_____

23. Explain the importance of modeling good moral behavior.

_____

_____

_____

_____

Name _____ Date _____ Class _____

Emotional Development
from Four to Six

Giving Constructive Feedback

Directions. Children from four to six are generally sensitive to criticism. Unsure of their abilities, they dislike being told that they did something wrong or need to improve. Read the following statements. In the spaces provided, write how you would rephrase the statement to make it more positive and constructive.

1. "You'll never get that tower of blocks to stay up if you don't work more carefully."

   _____

   _____

   _____

   _____

2. "I don't see any of the things you're describing in that picture. It just looks like a bunch of squiggles to me."

   _____

   _____

   _____

   _____

3. "You weren't picked for the team until last because you don't try hard enough." _____

   _____

   _____

   _____

   _____

4. "You mean you don't know how to tie your shoes yet?" _____

   _____

   _____

   _____

5. "Go clean your room, and do the whole job this time." _____

   _____

   _____

   _____

Social and Moral Development
from Four to Six

Teaching by Example

Directions: Read each of the case studies below. Then answer the questions that follow.

1. Terry Franklin woke up to the first day of spring weather. I can't imagine going in to the office today," he told his family at breakfast. "It's been such a long winter. I think I'll call in sick and enjoy this beautiful day!"

    A. What values did Terry show his children with this comment? _____

    _____

    B. What will his children learn from his actions? _____

    _____

    C. How do you think Terry would react if his children said they wanted to stay home from school because the weather was too nice?

    _____

    _____

2. Shane and his family were finishing up their picnic at the park. Five-year-old Shane was picking up their trash to throw it out when his sister said, "Don't bother. They have people who work here who come around and clean up. They'll take care of it."

    A. What values did Shane's sister show? _____

    _____

    _____

    B. What will Shane learn from her words and actions? _____

    _____

    _____

3. Six-year-old Jenny loves to draw and paint. Her father is happy that she likes art so much and proud of how well she draws. To give her materials to work with, he brought home blank paper and colored markers from the office.

    A. What values were shown by Jenny's father? _____

    _____

    B. What example did he set for Jenny? _____

    C. What do you think Jenny's father would say if she took something from a store? _____

    _____

    _____

(Continued on next page)

4. At dinner, Carly laughingly told the family how she and her friend had tricked their boss at work when she punched in her friend's time card an hour before her friend got to work.

   A. What values did Carly show? _____

   _____

   _____

   B. What example might her younger brother learn from her story? _____

   _____

   _____

5. Melissa and Kara claim they like to go to the mall to "people watch", as well as to shop. Sometimes they take their two young cousins along. "What is that guy doing with *her*?" Kara comments, looking at a couple she doesn't know. "She could stand to lose about 20 pounds and she definitely needs a better haircut."

   A. What values did Kara show? _____

   _____

   _____

   B. What example did she set for the young cousins? _____

   _____

   _____

6. Michelle's mother always scolded her for tattling or talking negatively about others. However, Michelle often heard her mother talking on the phone and the conversations often include unkind remarks about other people.

   A. Why do you think Michelle's mother says one thing but does the opposite? _____

   _____

   B. What effect might this have on how well Michelle minds her about other things? _____

   _____

   _____

Name _____ Date _____ Class _____

Intellectual Development from Four to Six

Study Guide

> **Directions.** Answer the following questions as you read the chapter. They will help you focus on the main points. Later, you can use this guide to review and study the chapter information.

Section 15–1: The Developing Brain from Four to Six

1. What does *IQ* stand for? How is the IQ number determined? _____
_____
_____

2. What IQ scores are considered average for children? _____

3. Why is the value of intelligence tests limited? _____
_____
_____
_____

4. Preschools and kindergartens typically use several techniques to assess children's development. Why?
_____
_____
_____

5. How might *cultural bias* affect intelligence testing? _____
_____
_____

6. How can caregivers and teachers use Gardner's theory of *multiple intelligences*? _____
_____
_____

7. After each of the phrases below, write the name of the kind of intelligence that is being described.
   A. Ability to imagine things visually and think in three dimensions. _____
   B. Ability to recognize and draw upon features of the environment. _____
   C. Ability to learn and use language. _____
   D. Ability to use the body to solve problems and to perform physical skills. _____
   _____
   E. Ability to understand oneself. _____
   F. Ability to understand other people. _____
   G. Ability to analyze problems and explore scientifically. _____
   H. Skill in performing and appreciating musical patterns. _____

(Continued on next page)

8. Summarize the thinking of children who are in Piaget's preoperational period. _____

_____

_____

_____

_____

9. Give an example (different from those in the text) of preoperational thinking among children ages four to six in each of the following areas:

A. Use of symbols: _____

_____

_____

B. Limited focus: _____

_____

_____

C. Make-believe play: _____

_____

_____

D. Egocentric viewpoint: _____

_____

_____

10. Sarah bombards her parents with questions such as "Why?" "How come?" and "Where?" Due to this behavior, how old do you think Sarah is?

_____

11. Compare the theories of Vygotsky and Montessori on how children learn. How are the theories similar? How are they different?

_____

_____

_____

_____

_____

_____

_____

(Continued on next page)

Section 15–2: Learning from Four to Six

12. Six-year-old Seth is drawing a picture with different colors of crayons. Write a comment that a caregiver could make that would promote self-esteem. Then write a question that would encourage Seth to organize his thoughts.

_____

_____

_____

_____

13. Carol is walking with her five-year-old grandson in the park. Write comments or questions that Carol could say that would promote learning.

_____

_____

_____

_____

14. Identify four drawbacks of too much television for children ages four to six.

_____

_____

_____

_____

_____

15. What are *phonemes*? What is a favorite type of book that helps children become more aware of phonemes?

_____

_____

_____

_____

16. What is *alliteration*? Is "babies bite bananas" an example of an alliteration? _____

_____

_____

17. Why do some children who are *bilingual* seem to have an advantage in reading over children who speak one language?

_____

_____

_____

_____

(Continued on next page)

18. What kinds of books or stories are four- to six-year-olds likely to enjoy? _____

_____

_____

_____

19. Give four examples of art materials that are appropriate for four- to six-year-olds. _____

_____

_____

_____

20. Holly is making something out of modeling clay. Her mother teases her by saying "What in the world is that supposed to be?" What could Holly's mother have said that would better promote learning and self-esteem?

_____

_____

_____

21. What are *finger plays*? _____

_____

22. Identify three common household items that children can use as musical instruments. _____

_____

_____

23. How does preschool help prepare children for kindergarten? _____

_____

_____

24. Identify three abilities that indicate that a child is ready to attend school. _____

_____

_____

_____

25. Cousins Josh and Tracy are both five years old. Josh started kindergarten, but Tracy has to wait until next year. Why do you think they weren't able to enroll together?

_____

_____

(Continued on next page)

Intellectual Development from Four to Six

26. Brad wants to give his son Nick an idea of what school will be like. What can Brad do?

_____

_____

27. What are some things parents can do to increase their child's feelings of independence before the child enters the unfamiliar world of school?

_____

_____

28. Children ages four to six improve dramatically in what two areas of language development?

_____

_____

29. Why are children able to say a word like "mop" sooner than a word like "please"? _____

_____

_____

_____

30. What are three reasons children may experience speech difficulties? _____

_____

_____

_____

_____

_____

The Developing Brain
from Four to Six

Identifying Theories of Intellectual Development

Directions: In this section, you studied the theories of intellectual development. The four researchers are listed in the box below. For each description or example in the chart that follows, identify the researcher whose theory it describes. Write the researcher's name in the space provided in the chart. Names may be used more than once.

Researchers

- Vygotsky
- Piaget
- Montessori
- Gardner

Researchers	Descriptions or Examples
	1. Children move through a series of learning stages as they develop intellectually.
	2. Learning occurs in, and depends on, the social environment.
	3. Children learn naturally if placed in a prepared learning environment containing appropriate materials.
	4. Children between ages two and seven can view the world only from their own perspective.
	5. Each person has a blend of intelligences.
	6. Teachers should collaborate with students rather than lecturing them.
	7. Teachers should allow students a great deal of independence and never interrupt a student engaged in a task.
	8. If caregivers recognize that a child is high in one type of intelligence, they can provide learning opportunities to build on that strength.

Name _____ Date _____ Class _____

Learning from Four to Six

Adjusting to School

Directions: The situations below describe children who are starting school. If the parents' words and actions will help the child adjust to school, write **"Yes"** in the blank to the left of the number. In the space below the description, explain why. If the parents' actions and words will *not* help the child adjust to school, write **"No"** in the blank and suggest a better approach in the spaces provided.

_____ **1.** Ethan turned five just before the school district's birthday cut-off date for starting school. Still, Ethan's parents were unsure about enrolling him. He would be among the youngest in his class. His grandparents claim that he's very bright for his age. However, his attention span is short, and he has trouble following directions. His parents decide to wait until next year to enroll Ethan in kindergarten.

_____

_____

_____

_____ **2.** The week before Katie was going to school, she and her mother shopped for school supplies. They followed the list that the teacher had sent home. Katie picked things in the colors that she wanted. When they got home, she put them in her school bag. Every day she took things out and looked at them, waiting for school to begin.

_____

_____

_____

_____ **3.** The week before school started, Andrew started to have trouble sleeping. He had always gone to bed easily, but he began to insist that one of his parents stay with him. They were both very busy, though, and told him he had to go to sleep on his own.

_____

_____

_____

_____

(Continued on next page)

Copyright © Glencoe/McGraw-Hill
a division of The McGraw-Hill Companies, Inc.

The Developing Child: **Student Activity Manual** **129**

_____ **4.** Every day, when Shemika gets home from school, she and her mother argue. She wants to play outside, but her mother says she should do her homework first. "You should finish your work before having fun," her mother says. Shemika pouts and cries.

_____

_____

_____

_____

_____ **5.** All during August, Domnick asked his older sister what school was like. Finally, his mother took him to visit the school. They walked around to see the other rooms and looked at the kindergarten classroom. They met the teacher, who was preparing the room for the new year. Domnick's name was already on the bulletin board.

_____

_____

_____

_____

_____ **6.** As the summer came to a close, Ashley's parents often talked about school. Her mother said, "It will be so lonely here without you." Her father said, "It will be a big adjustment for you, little girl. You won't be able to sleep late. You'll miss your TV shows. You'll be away from home all day long. That's OK, though, because you'll have fun."

_____

_____

_____

_____

_____ **7.** Antonio will start kindergarten next week, and he is showing signs of anxiety. He is timid about meeting new people. Antonio loves to play kickball. Antonio's mother arranged a play day in the local park. She invited several children who will be in Antonio's class to come to the park to play kickball and other games.

_____

_____

_____

_____

_____

Physical Development from Seven to Twelve

Study Guide

Directions. Answer the following questions as you read the chapter. They will help you focus on the main points. Later, you can use this guide to review and study the chapter information.

Section 16–1: Growth and Development from Seven to Twelve

1. Describe how average height and weight change for children at the following ages.

   A. Seven to Ten: _____

   _____

   _____

   _____

   B. Eleven to Twelve: _____

   _____

   _____

   _____

2. Why are eleven- and twelve-year-old girls typically taller than boys their age? _____

   _____

   _____

3. What factor has the most influence on a child's ultimate height? _____

   _____

4. What factors may cause preteen girls to be sensitive about their *body image*? _____

   _____

5. What is the definition of an *eating disorder*? _____

   _____

6. How can participation in organized sports benefit children in this age group? _____

   _____

   _____

7. What is *scoliosis*? How is it treated? _____

   _____

   _____

(Continued on next page)

The Developing Child: **Student Activity Manual**

8. At about what age does the second set of molars emerge? What is another name for a third set of molars?

   _____

9. Identify at least five physical changes that occur in boys and five that occur in girls during puberty.

   A. Boys: _____

   _____

   _____

   _____

   _____

   _____

   B. Girls: _____

   _____

   _____

   _____

   _____

   _____

10. What is *menstruation*? At about what age does it begin? _____

    _____

    _____

    _____

11. What physical development in the years from seven to twelve enable motor skills to improve?

    _____

Section 16–2: Caring for Children from Seven to Twelve

12. Why are the Dietary Guidelines for Americans helpful for both children and adults? _____

    _____

    _____

13. What foods contain fiber? Why is fiber important in a healthy diet? _____

    _____

    _____

14. Where should most fats come from in a healthy diet? _____

    _____

(Continued on next page)

Physical Development from Seven to Twelve   **Chapter 16 continued**

15. Name four things that families can do to encourage good eating habits for children. _____

_____

_____

_____

_____

_____

16. What link have researchers found between eating breakfast and classroom performance?

_____

_____

_____

17. Describe each of the following *eating disorders*.

   A. Anorexia nervosa: _____

   _____

   B. Bulimia: _____

   _____

   C. Binge eating: _____

   _____

18. What emotional or psychological problems characterize many children with eating disorders?

_____

_____

19. Which of the following are *sedentary activities*—jumping on a trampoline, watching a DVD, playing a board game, or walking a dog? Explain.

_____

_____

20. Seven-year-old Nate wants to play ice hockey like some friends, but his father wants to sign him up for golf lessons. What would you do if you were his parent?

_____

_____

_____

_____

21. How much physical activity is recommended for children and teens each day? _____

_____

22. About how many hours of sleep should school-age children get each night? _____

_____

(Continued on next page)

23. Explain how tooth decay occurs, and how sugary foods and drinks contribute to it. _____

_____

_____

_____

24. What are *sealants* on children's teeth? _____

_____

25. Why do some parents arrange for their children to see an *orthodontist*? _____

_____

26. List at least four principles that children should be taught about personal safety. _____

_____

_____

_____

_____

_____

27. How do physical changes during puberty require preteens to adopt different personal hygiene habits than when they were younger?

_____

_____

_____

_____

_____

_____

28. What vaccines are usually required for children entering fifth grade? _____

_____

_____

_____

_____

*Growth and Development
from Seven to Twelve*

A Time of Change

Directions: Nine children and preteens attend a latchkey program at the Oak Street Community Center. Volunteers help with homework, supervise games, and provide snacks. Today is "health day" and those who attend can be weighed and measured if they wish. Using your textbook, estimate the children's ages based on the information given. Assume that the children are average for their age.

1. Dustin weighs 71 pounds and is 54 inches tall. He is _____ years old.

2. Seth weighs 55 pounds and is 51 inches tall. He is _____ years old.

3. Grace complains that her mouth hurts because her second molars are coming in. She is _____ years old.

4. Sierra weighs 48 pounds and is 48 inches tall. She is _____ years old.

5. Kristen is surprised that she has gained 10 pounds since last year when she weighed 72 pounds. She is 57 inches tall. Kristen is _____ years old. Her weight gain is [normal; average] for her age.

6. Alejandro is almost 5 feet tall and weighs 90 pounds. He is _____ years old.

7. Tanner's height has increased from 52 inches to 57 inches. The program volunteer says, "You must be in a growth [spurt]! Tanner weighs 80 pounds. He is _____ years old.

8. A nurse detects that Alejandro's spine seems to curve slightly. He should be checked for _____

9. Molly is 53 inches tall and weighs 67 pounds. She is _____ years old.

10. Zach is nine years old. His height is 52 inches. How much might you expect him to weigh? _____ _____

Directions: Answer the questions in the space provided.

11. Why do preteens vary so much in size, from one to another? _____
_____

12. Why do you think preteen girls are at higher risk for eating disorders than when they were younger?
_____
_____

13. Do you think the benefits of team sports outweigh their possible drawbacks? Explain your point of view.
_____
_____

Name _____ Date _____ Class _____

Caring for Children
from Seven to Twelve

SECTION 16–2

Adjusting to a Changing Body

Directions: Take the role of "Dear Chris," a columnist who offers advice to children and preteens. Read the following letters and then write your responses in the spaces provided.

Dear Chris,
You've got to help me. I'm eleven, and I'm gaining too much weight. No matter how little I eat, my clothes feel tighter and tighter. I figure my only choice is to eat nothing but celery and carrot sticks. Vegetables are healthy, right?

_____
_____
_____
_____
_____
_____
_____

Dear Chris,
My favorite teacher got on me for not participating. She said that my grades are slipping. I don't know what it is. I can't seem to concentrate anymore. I'm too tired to focus, even though I get almost eight hours of sleep most nights.

_____
_____
_____
_____
_____
_____
_____

Dear Chris,
I have to wash my hair every day or it looks gross by sixth period. It takes me half an hour to dry it now, so I have to wake up extra early. What gives?

_____
_____
_____
_____
_____
_____
_____

Dear Chris,
I hate the way my voice sounds. There's a girl I want to talk to, but I'm afraid that my voice will crack and she'll laugh at me. What can I do?

_____
_____
_____
_____
_____
_____
_____

*Emotional and Social Development
from Seven to Twelve*

Study Guide

Directions. Answer the following questions as you read the chapter. They will help you focus on the main points. Later, you can use this guide to review and study the chapter information.

Section 17–1: Emotional Development from Seven to Twelve

1. Identify three signs that children between the ages of seven and twelve are developing a *sense of self*.

_____

_____

_____

_____

_____

_____

_____

2. How is the development of a *sense of competence* related to self-esteem? _____

_____

_____

3. Why is it important for children ages seven to twelve to experience more successes than failures?

_____

_____

_____

_____

4. Identify four strategies you could use to help a child develop a sense of competence. _____

_____

_____

_____

_____

5. Describe three signs that *gender identity* is being strengthened in children ages seven to twelve.

_____

_____

_____

_____

(Continued on next page)

6. Kaleel is curious and loves to explore. When he makes a discovery, he tells exaggerated tales of his exploits. Kaleel is showing characteristics of what age?

_____

7. Maya is absorbed in her own thoughts. Her moods change frequently. She often ignores others, seeming not to care what they say. Is Maya more likely in middle childhood or in the preteen years?

_____

8. By what age do children generally understand that they should express their anger in socially acceptable ways?

_____

9. Suggest a way to help an angry child regain self-control. _____

_____

_____

_____

_____

10. How do children's fears generally change between the ages of seven and twelve? _____

_____

_____

_____

_____

_____

_____

_____

11. How is normal *anxiety* different from an anxiety disorder? _____

_____

_____

_____

_____

_____

12. How might children these ages express envy? _____

_____

_____

13. Identify four strategies for living with seven- to twelve-year-olds. _____

_____

_____

_____

_____

(Continued on next page)

Section 17–2: Social and Moral Development from Seven to Twelve

14. What qualities become important in friendships around age seven or eight? _____

_____

_____

_____

15. What role do peer groups play in the self-esteem of older children and preteens? _____

_____

_____

_____

16. Why is the number of friends a child has not a good indicator that the child has a healthy social life? What is a better way of evaluating this?

_____

_____

_____

_____

_____

_____

17. Describe a four-step process for helping preteens resolve conflicts with peers. _____

_____

_____

_____

_____

18. Why do victims of *bullying* often hide the problem from adults? What should a parent or caregiver do to help?

_____

_____

_____

_____

_____

_____

(Continued on next page)

19. How and why do relationships between children and parents change during middle childhood and the preteen years?

_____

_____

_____

20. How can parents help a child make moral choices when the parents are not around? _____

_____

_____

_____

_____

21. Why is *peer pressure* strong during preteen years? How does it lead to *conformity*? _____

_____

_____

_____

_____

_____

22. Describe three ways that preteens can avoid negative peer pressure. _____

_____

_____

_____

_____

_____

23. Give an example of a low-risk decision that parents can allow preteens to make to encourage responsibility.

_____

_____

_____

24. What are two effective forms of punishment for preteens who break family rules? _____

_____

_____

*Emotional Development
from Seven to Twelve*

Recognizing Characteristic Behaviors

Directions. For each statement below, choose the age at which the behavior or development is *most* typical. Write the correct age in the space to the left of the statement. *You may use answers more than once.*

Ages	
Seven	Ten
Eight	Eleven and twelve
Nine	

Ages	Behaviors
_____	1. Typical of her generally happy outlook on life, Alexia is no longer worried by nighttime fears.
_____	2. Ryan's parents can't believe the change. Last year, he had been quiet and seemed never to want to leave the house. This year, he is outgoing and confident and is out playing every chance he can.
_____	3. Allison sits by herself, hardly saying a word to others. At night, though, she likes her mother's company because she is afraid of the dark.
_____	4. In earlier years, Luke referred to himself as Miranda's brother, but now when he talks about himself he describes what kind of person he is. "I like to laugh," he says, or "I'm honest."
_____	5. Abby is so caught up in thinking about how embarrassed she was at school that she doesn't even hear her father call to say that dinner is ready.
_____	6. "It's funny," Kendall says to his friend Samir. "The people at school think I'm one kind of person and the people in the karate school think I'm totally another kind of person."
_____	7. Anthony wants to tell his family what happened at school today. He describes the whole scene, speaking in an excited voice and waving his arms as he talks.
_____	8. Julia is frustrated because her friend Amy is spending more time with another classmate. When she gets home from school and her mother asks her to pick up her things, she refuses.
_____	9. Vincent seems to worry all the time, and he finds it very difficult to accept any criticism.
_____	10. Sarah's parents are worried about her. She seems to be very harsh on herself whenever she makes a mistake.

Social and Moral Development
from Seven to Twelve

Setting Rules and Responsibilities

Part 1 Directions: You are the parent of twelve-year-old Kirsten. You want to establish rules and responsibilities for Kirsten that are reasonable and appropriate for her age. In the chart below, write the rules or responsibilities you would set for each category.

Category	Rule or Responsibility
Homework	
Attending parties	
Household chores	

Part 2 Directions: Below are descriptions of Kirsten's behaviors. In the spaces that follow each description, write your response to the behavior.

1. Kirsten arrives home a half-hour late from a party. "My curfew is too strict," she says. "I'm embarrassed when I have to leave an hour earlier than everyone else."

    _____

    _____

2. On a school night, Kirsten watches a television show until midnight. _____

    _____

3. One evening, Kirsten comes home early from a party. "I was not comfortable," she said. "Some people were secretly drinking beer."

    _____

    _____

Name _____ Date _____ Class _____

Intellectual Development from
Seven to Twelve

Study Guide

Directions. Answer the following questions as you read the chapter. They will help you focus on the main points. Later, you can use this guide to review and study the chapter information.

Section 18–1: The Developing Brain from Seven to Twelve

1. What are the two types of memory? _____

2. At about what age do children begin to understand another person's point of view? _____

3. How do preteens view complex social problems, such as prejudice or poverty? _____
   _____
   _____
   _____
   _____

4. What happens to a child's attention span at about age twelve? How does this affect learning?
   _____
   _____
   _____

5. Imagine that a nine-year-old is sorting through a toy box of stuffed animals. Give an example of the child classifying objects, placing objects in a series, exhibiting the use of *transitivity*, or *conservation*. Then summarize the intellectual development of children ages seven to ten in each of those areas.

   A. Classifying objects: _____
   _____

   B. Placing objects in a series: _____
   _____

   C. Transitivity: _____
   _____

   D. Conservation: _____
   _____
   _____

6. What is the difference between the thinking skills of seven-year-olds and preteens?
   _____
   _____
   _____
   _____

(Continued on next page)

7. What is meant by a *hypothetical situation*? In which of Piaget's stages is a child capable of imagining such situations?

_____

_____

8. What did Piaget consider to be the basis for his learning stages? Compare Piaget's view of learning with Vygotsky's theory.

_____

_____

_____

_____

9. Contrast Montessori's view of learning with Vygotsky's theory. _____

_____

_____

_____

_____

10. How does Gardner's view of intelligence differ from Piaget's view? _____

_____

_____

_____

_____

_____

11. Abigail faithfully writes in her diary on a daily basis. Based on this activity, which one of Gardner's multiple intelligences is one of her strengths?

_____

12. What are the three types of intelligence proposed by Robert Sternberg's theory? Children who are gifted in music and art would likely rate high in which type?

_____

_____

_____

_____

_____

(Continued on next page)

Intellectual Development from Seven to Twelve　　　　　　*Chapter 18 continued*

Section 18–2: Learning from Seven to Twelve

13. Why is direct learning effective for older children? How is direct learning different from *learning methods* used for children who are just starting school?

_____

_____

_____

_____

14. How might a teacher encourage *peer learning*? _____

_____

_____

15. How might a teacher help fifth- or sixth-graders gain the independent learning skills they need to complete a long-term project?

_____

_____

_____

_____

16. In what way is the structure of middle school like elementary school? How is it like high school?

_____

_____

_____

_____

17. How are *standardized tests* developed? _____

_____

_____

_____

18. Explain each of the following properties of good standardized tests.

A. Validity: _____

_____

_____

B. Reliability: _____

_____

_____

C. Practicality: _____

_____

_____

(Continued on next page)

19. What do each of the following standardized tests measure?

    A. Learning ability tests: _____

    _____

    _____

    B. Achievement tests: _____

    _____

    _____

    C. Aptitude and interest tests: _____

    _____

    _____

20. Identify two possible limitations of standardized tests. _____

_____

_____

_____

_____

_____

_____

21. How are standardized test scores used? _____

_____

_____

_____

_____

(Continued on next page)

The Developing Child: **Student Activity Manual**

Name _____ Date _____ Class _____

*The Developing Brain
from Seven to Twelve*

Identifying Categories of Intelligence

Part 1 Directions: The following box lists the different types of intelligence identified by Howard Gardner. For each activity described below, identify the type of intelligence the activity would help develop in a child.

Types of Intelligence

Bodily-kinesthetic	Logical-mathematical	Verbal-linguistic
Interpersonal	Musical	Visual-spatial
Intrapersonal	Naturalistic	

_____ 1. Brett was chosen to lead the planning committee for the class car wash.

_____ 2. Evan helped paint a mural of school activities to display at the community's centennial celebration.

_____ 3. Brooke's experiment with magnetism won a ribbon at the science fair.

_____ 4. For the school's talent show, Savannah created rhythms using pots, spoons, and other common items as instruments.

_____ 5. Iola read the children's story she wrote to the kindergarten class.

_____ 6. During his summer vacation, Logan recorded his feelings about his experiences in a journal.

_____ 7. The class visited a local park to learn about plants and birds in their area.

_____ 8. At soccer practice, Austin learned how to perform a corner kick.

Part 2 Directions: Using Sternberg's categories of intelligence identify whether each child described below is high in **creative**, **practical**, or **analytical** intelligence.

_____ 9. Sean's grades are not the best, but when he and his friends hit a snag in building their tree house, Sean easily figured out a solution.

_____ 10. Kiesha is the class brain. She always seems to get the best grades on tests.

_____ 11. Tori doesn't do well in school. She seldom follows the teacher's instructions. However, she loves to paint.

_____ 12. Jill's design suggestion was used for the poster advertising the school play.

_____ 13. Michael and Lori were chosen to represent the school at the regional math competition.

_____ 14. Maurice came up with a plan for a peer-tutoring program for school.

_____ 15. Lucy pointed out to the group that the solution they were discussing failed to solve the problem in the past.

Name _____ Date _____ Class _____

Learning and Assessment Methods

Part 1 Directions: In the diagram below, identify three learning methods that are appropriate for the seven-to-twelve age group. For each method, give an example of an assignment that uses the method. Give different examples from those in the textbook.

Learning Methods

Method:	Method:	Method:

Example:	Example:	Example:

Part 2 Directions: Each description below relates to one of three types of standardized tests: **achievement** tests, **aptitude and interest** tests, or **learning ability** tests. Complete the chart by writing the type of test in the left column next to its description. Test types may be used more than once.

Type of Standardized Test	Description
	Scores can help students determine the kinds of careers that might be right for them.
	Tests of this type are sometimes known as IQ tests.
	A test of this type may ask students to select what they like best from different groups of ideas or activities.
	A certain score on this type of test may be required for graduation.
	A test of this type may measure what students have learned about biology, for example.

Adolescence

Study Guide

> **Directions.** Answer the following questions as you read the chapter. They will help you focus on the main points. Later, you can use this guide to review and study the chapter information.

Section 19–1: Physical Development of Adolescents

1. Summarize the general pattern of growth for adolescents. How does the pattern differ between males and females?

   _____

   _____

   _____

   _____

   _____

2. What physical changes occur as a girl's body increases its production of *estrogen*? _____

   _____

   _____

3. What is *testosterone*? How does it relate to puberty? _____

   _____

   _____

   _____

   _____

4. How does puberty impact nutritional needs? _____

   _____

   _____

   _____

5. Why are personal cleanliness routines particularly important for adolescents? _____

   _____

   _____

   _____

6. How can regular exercise benefit teens? _____

   _____

   _____

   _____

   _____

(Continued on next page)

7. Give three negative effects that teens may experience if they do not get enough sleep. _____

_____

_____

_____

Section 19–2: Emotional and Social Development of Adolescents

8. What is *personal identity*? _____

_____

9. Describe how the following factors influence identity development.

A. Family: _____

_____

_____

B. Peers: _____

_____

_____

C. The future: _____

_____

_____

10. According to Erik Erikson, what is an *identity crisis*? How is it related to conformity? _____

_____

_____

_____

11. Summarize four paths to a sense of *personal identity* that teens may explore, according to James Marcia.

_____

_____

_____

_____

_____

(Continued on next page)

12. Identify three warning signs of *depression*. If you see these signs in a teen, what should you do?

_____
_____
_____
_____
_____
_____

13. Describe four possible symptoms of anxiety. If the problem is not addressed, what further problems may result?

_____
_____
_____
_____
_____
_____

14. Describe the two extremes characteristic of *bipolar disorder*. _____

_____
_____
_____

15. How can teens' desire for independence lead to problems in the family? _____

_____
_____

16. What role does a close friend play in a teen's life? _____

_____
_____

17. Why is it important for teens to participate in a variety of activities? _____

_____
_____

(Continued on next page)

Section 19–3: Moral Development of Adolescents

18. What is a "moral compass"? _____

19. Why do teens need to develop a reliable moral compass? _____
_____
_____

20. According to Kohlberg, what increases as a person progresses through the six stages of moral development?
_____

21. How does Kohlberg define *moral maturity*? _____
_____

22. What positive effects can peer groups have on teens? _____
_____
_____
_____

23. Why do some teens get involved in drugs, drinking, and other negative behaviors? _____
_____
_____
_____
_____

24. Give two examples of ways that *popular culture* might negatively influence teen behaviors.
_____
_____

25. How can parents promote *morality* and positive values in teens? Identify at least three ways.
_____
_____
_____
_____

26. What are some of the potential consequences for teens who lack a strong set of personal values?
_____
_____
_____
_____

(Continued on next page)

Section 19–4: Intellectual Development of Adolescents

27. What part of the brain undergoes the most dramatic changes during adolescence? What are its functions?

_____

_____

_____

28. What functions does the *amygdala* control? What kinds of actions result when teens use this part of the brain more than the thinking part?

_____

_____

_____

29. What happens to brain connections during adolescence? What does this indicate about the importance of intellectual pursuits during this time?

_____

_____

_____

_____

30. How does a teen's intellect change once he or she is capable of *abstract thought*? _____

_____

_____

_____

31. Describe two criticisms of Piaget's four-stage theory. _____

_____

_____

_____

32. In what major way did Vygotsky's beliefs differ from Piaget's? _____

_____

_____

33. What did Vygotsky believe students needed to reach the heights of their potential? _____

_____

_____

34. Describe some of the factors that can help a student learn more in school. _____

_____

_____

_____

Physical Development of Adolescents

Developing Health Habits

> **Directions:** You are the parent of Josh, age 13. Read the descriptions of some of Josh's behaviors. In the space below each description, write what you would say or do to guide Josh toward more healthful habits.

1. Every Friday, Cheesecakes Galore sponsors an all-you-can-eat buffet of desserts. Josh and his friends seldom miss this event.

   _____

   _____

   _____

   _____

2. Since he was ten, Josh has been taking showers every day. Now that he is an adolescent, you notice more body odor between showers.

   _____

   _____

   _____

   _____

3. Josh got in-line skates last year and usually skated with his friend Diego after school. Now, he and Diego are playing video games instead.

   _____

   _____

   _____

   _____

4. After Josh completes his homework, he watches television until 11:00 p.m. He says TV relaxes him. When you wake him at 6:00 a.m. to get ready for school, Josh is groggy and irritable. He has complained of difficulty concentrating in school.]

   _____

   _____

   _____

   _____

   _____

The Developing Child: **Student Activity Manual**

Emotional and Social Development
of Adolescents

Recognizing Emotional Warning Signs

Directions: For each situation described below, judge whether the teen's behavior is normal or a warning sign of an emotional problem. Write **Normal** or **Warning** in the space to the left of the description to indicate your assessment. In the spaces below each description, explain why you judged the behavior to be normal or a sign of a problem.

_____ 1. Amanda's parents are concerned. Amanda seems moody and often is so absorbed in her own thoughts that she hardly talks to her family. When her friends ask her to do something she enjoys, she brightens up.

_____

_____

_____

_____

_____ 2. Cory's friends are not sure what to think. When they go to the movies or to the mall, Cory refuses to go with them. He won't even to go parties if a lot of people will be there. "Crowds are a hassle," Cory says.

_____

_____

_____

_____

_____ 3. While driving home from school on Friday, seventeen-year-old Jennifer chatters excitedly to her friends about her latest adventure as she weaves fearlessly through traffic. The next week, she doesn't want to drive and she stays home from school even though it means she will miss tryouts for the talent show.

_____

_____

_____

_____

_____

_____

(Continued on next page)

The Developing Child: **Student Activity Manual**

_____   **4.** Manuel just broke up with his girlfriend. He is sitting on his front porch staring into space when his friend Dustin arrives. Dustin suggests that they play basketball. "Maybe shooting hoops will help me feel better," Manuel says. "Let's go."

_____

_____

_____

_____

_____   **5.** "What's wrong with me?" seventeen-year-old Dante wondered. "I feel very sad most of the time and just don't want to do anything. I don't even like to play video games anymore."

_____

_____

_____

_____

_____   **6.** Ashley sits in a corner as the party goes on around her. Making friends at her new school isn't easy for her. She wishes that she could just blend into the wall so that no one will notice her. She goes in the bathroom and takes a bottle of wine from her bag. "At least this drink will help me get through this," she says to herself.

_____

_____

_____

_____

_____   **7.** Erik's parents don't know what to think. Erik has always been cooperative. Now, though, his attitude is changing. He doesn't seem to agree with them on anything. He wears strange, secondhand clothes and got his ear pierced without their permission. When his mother buys him new clothes for school, they just sit in the shopping bag.

_____

_____

_____

_____

Moral Development of Adolescents

Kohlberg's Stages of Moral Development

Directions: In the diagram below, describe each stage of moral development according to Lawrence Kohlberg's theory. Along the diagonal arrow, indicate what increases as a person progresses through the six stages.

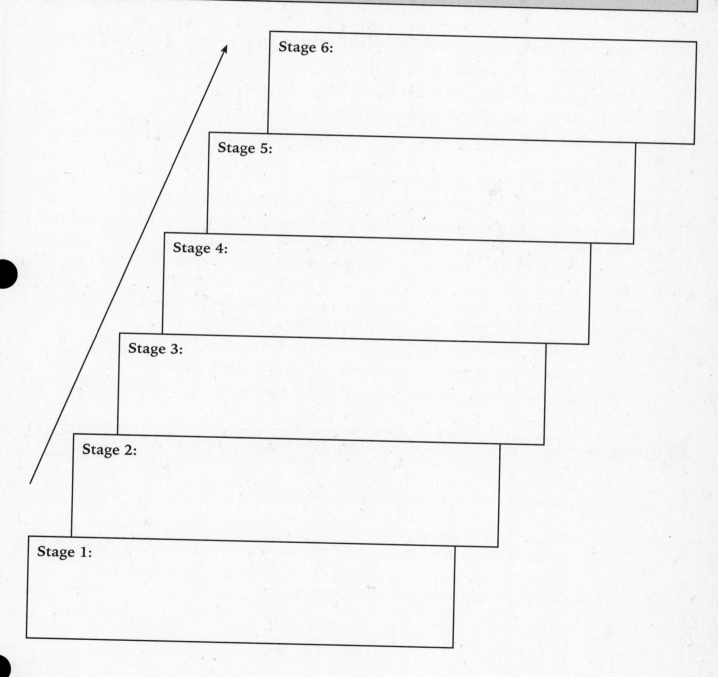

Stage 6:

Stage 5:

Stage 4:

Stage 3:

Stage 2:

Stage 1:

The Developing Child: **Student Activity Manual**

Emotional and Social Development
of Adolescents

SECTION 19–4

Influences on Intellectual Development

Directions: Read the following sentences. Underline the word or phrase inside the parentheses that best completes the statement.

1. The brain starts to grow again just (before, after) puberty.

2. The maturing of the (prefrontal cortex, amygdala) makes it possible for teens to reason better.

3. The (prefrontal cortex, amygdala) is responsible for emotional reactions, such as fear and joy.

4. The (prefrontal cortex, amygdala) is located just behind the forehead.

5. Teens' brains make (more, fewer) connections than they actually need.

6. Piaget called his fourth and final stage of intellectual development the (formal, concrete) operations stage.

7. According to Piaget, children enter this fourth stage around age (11, 14).

8. During the fourth stage, young people become capable of (moral, abstract) thought.

9. (Piaget, Vygotsky) believed that children develop the ability to think by interacting with parents, teachers, and peers.

10. According to Vygotsky, the "zone of proximal development" is a measure of a child's learning (achievement, potential).

11. Vygotsky believed that students could achieve their greatest learning potential only through (self-directed activities, collaboration with teachers and other students).

12. Students who (fear, respect) their teachers are more willing to learn.

13. More learning occurs when students have a (positive, negative) attitude about school.

14. Teens generally (want, don't want) their parents to take an active interest in their education.

Directions: Answer each of the following questions in the space provided.

15. Describe what your positive learning environment would be like. _____

_____

_____

16. Explain how you believe parents can best encourage learning. _____

_____

_____

Name _____ Date _____ Class _____

Children's Health and Safety

CHAPTER 20

Study Guide

> **Directions:** Answer the following questions as you read the chapter. They will help you focus on the main points. Later, you can use this guide to review and study the chapter information.

Section 20–1: Childhood Illnesses

1. How can regular medical checkups help prevent serious illnesses? _____
_____
_____

2. Identify at least three symptoms in young children that indicate the need to call the child's doctor.
_____
_____
_____

3. What is a *communicable disease*? _____

4. What does it mean to be "allergic" to something? What are the symptoms of an allergic reaction?
_____
_____
_____

5. Identify three foods and three airborne substances that are commonly known to cause allergic reactions in children.
_____
_____
_____
_____

6. What role does heredity play in allergies? _____
_____
_____

7. How can allergies be treated? _____
_____
_____

(Continued on next page)

8. What occurs in the body during an *asthma* attack? What are the signs of an attack? _____
_____
_____
_____
_____

9. What can bring on an asthma attack? _____
_____
_____

10. What is the *contagious* period of an illness? Why should children be kept at home during this time?
_____
_____
_____
_____

11. Why is it important never to give aspirin to a child with a fever? _____
_____
_____
_____

12. When an unhappy baby is crying and pulling on his or her ear, what might parents suspect? What action should they take?
_____
_____

13. Describe ways to comfort a sick child. _____
_____
_____
_____
_____

14. Why is it important that children take in plenty of liquids while they are ill? _____
_____
_____

15. How can parents prepare a child for a planned hospitalization? _____
_____
_____
_____

(Continued on next page)

Section 20–2: Accidents and Emergencies

16. Melissa will be babysitting her neighbor's children for the summer. How could she prepare for the possibility of a fire?

_____

_____

_____

_____

17. What are the five guidelines for action in case of an accident? _____

_____

_____

_____

18. When caregivers of an injured child call for help, what kinds of information should they provide?

_____

_____

_____

_____

19. Describe the correct first-aid procedure for each of the following:

Problem	Procedure
Bruise	
First-degree burn	
Minor cut or scrape	
Sprained ankle	
Nosebleed	
Chemical burn	

(Continued on next page)

20. How is a *fracture* different from a *sprain*? How are they similar? _____

_____

_____

_____

_____

21. How can you tell a second-degree burn from a first-degree burn? _____

_____

_____

22. What are the signs of choking? Why must the caregiver act quickly? _____

_____

_____

_____

_____

23. Describe the technique a caregiver should try first to help a choking infant. _____

_____

_____

_____

_____

24. What is another name for a *convulsion*? What occurs during a convulsion? What should be put in a child's mouth during a convulsion?

_____

_____

_____

_____

25. What do *hives* look like? What should the caregiver do if a child develops hives after a bee sting? Why?

_____

_____

26. Elisa's three-year-old was having difficulty breathing. She noticed burns around his mouth and his breath smelled strange. What might this indicate? What should she do?

_____

_____

(Continued on next page)

Children's Health and Safety

27. What are the symptoms of *shock*? How should a caregiver treat an injured child who may be in shock?

_____

_____

_____

_____

_____

_____

_____

_____

28. During *rescue breathing*, what is the purpose of lifting the child's chin with one hand and pushing down on the forehead with the other?

_____

29. When are the following rescue techniques used?

A. Rescue breathing: _____

B. *CPR*: _____

Childhood Illnesses   **SECTION 20–1**

Identifying Childhood Diseases

> **Directions:** Several common disease symptoms are described below. In the space provided, identify the probable disease, describe the treatment, and indicate whether any medication can be given to the child.

1. Symptoms: Runny nose, sneezing, coughing, mild fever, sore throat **Disease:** **Treatment:** **Medication:**	**2. Symptoms:** Coughing, wheezing, rapid breathing, shortness of breath **Disease:** **Treatment:** **Medication:**
3. Symptoms: Rash of tiny red pimples that develop into blisters, low fever **Disease:** **Treatment:** **Medication:**	**4. Symptoms:** High fever, chills, shakes, body ache **Disease:** **Treatment:** **Medication:**
5. Symptoms: Fever, headache, sore throat without runny nose or congestion, white patches on tonsils, red rash **Disease:** **Treatment:** **Medication:**	**6. Symptoms:** Fever, pulling at ear **Disease:** **Treatment:** **Medication:**

Accidents and Emergencies

Taking the Right Steps in an Emergency

Directions: Listed below are several emergency situations. After each situation is a set of steps that should be followed. The steps are in the wrong order, however. Put them in the correct order by writing the number from 1 to 5 in the spaces to the left of steps.

1. Luisa enters the kitchen and finds her little brother Manuel lying on the floor unconscious. Next to him is an open bottle of cleanser, knocked over.

   _____ Take Manuel to the hospital, as directed.

   _____ Look at the label on the bottle to see if the cleanser is poisonous.

   _____ Call the poison control center.

   _____ Bring the bottle to the phone.

   _____ Smell Manuel's breath to see if he swallowed any of the cleanser.

2. Shelley is babysitting five-year-old Matt and three-year-old Chelsea. The children are playing in the backyard. Shelley hears Matt cry out in pain and come running. He says that a bee stung him.

   _____ Apply cold pack.

   _____ Wash area with soap and water.

   _____ Scrape off the stinger.

   _____ Watch for signs on an allergic reaction or infection.

   _____ Give acetaminophen for pain.

3. Leon's nine-month-old sister is happily eating a snack when suddenly he notices that he's not hearing her babbling any more. Leon looks over and sees his sister's head leaning to the side of the high chair, and she is waving her hands in the air.

   _____ Use the heel of his hand to give up to five quick blows between her shoulder blades.

   _____ If object is not expelled, place two fingers on middle of breastbone just below nipples and give up to five quick downward thrusts.

   _____ Go to his sister and pick her up.

   _____ Put her face down over his arm, holding her jaw in his fingers.

   _____ Turn her face up.

4. Madison is out riding her tricycle when she crashes. Sobbing, she shows her father that her knee is scraped and bloody.

   _____ Place a clean gauze bandage on the wound and press for several minutes to stop the bleeding.

   _____ Cover the wound with an antiseptic ointment.

   _____ Wash the area with mild soap and warm water.

   _____ Put a clean bandage over the wound.

   _____ Pat the area dry with a clean towel.

(Continued on next page)

5. Erica finds her little son face down in the pool. She takes him out and lays him on the lawn of the backyard. He is not breathing.

_____ Turn his head face up, lift the chin with one hand and push down on the forehead with the other.

_____ If her son's chest rises, remove her mouth and let his lungs expel air. Then repeat.

_____ Take a deep breath.

_____ Put her mouth over the mouth of her son, pinching her son's nostrils shut, and blow air into her son's mouth.

_____ Put her son on his back, turn his head to one side, and try to get rid of any water in his mouth.

6. Ryan's ten-year-old daughter Hannah was eating a piece of hard candy. Suddenly, she started choking. By the time he realized what was happening, she had fallen down and started to lose consciousness.

_____ If the object cannot be removed, place the heal of one hand in the middle of Hannah's abdomen just above the navel, and place the other hand on top of the first hand.

_____ Check Hannah's mouth again to see if the candy can be removed.

_____ Put Hannah on her back.

_____ Give five quick thrusts, pressing both hands in and up.

_____ Check Hannah's mouth for the candy and try to remove it with a sweeping motion of Ryan's index finger.

Family Challenges

CHAPTER 21

Study Guide

> **Directions:** Answer the following questions as you read the chapter. They will help you focus on the main points. Later, you can use this guide to review and study the chapter information.

Section 21–1: Family Stresses

1. After his parents divorced, Josh, age three began snatching his baby sister's bottle and drinking from it. What sign of stress is Josh displaying?

   _____

2. Identify three signs of stress in children under the age of five. _____

   _____

   _____

   _____

3. Identify three signs of stress in teens. _____

   _____

   _____

   _____

4. Give four examples of family situations that commonly cause *situational stress* in children.

   _____

   _____

   _____

   _____

5. What can parents do after a move to help children adjust? _____

   _____

6. Should children be told of family financial problems? Why or why not? _____

   _____

   _____

   _____

   _____

7. How should parents tell their children that they are going to divorce? _____

   _____

   _____

(Continued on next page)

8. If children will go back and forth between homes after a divorce, how can the parents help them feel comfortable at each home?

_____

_____

_____

9. How can *support groups* help families of substance abusers? _____

_____

_____

_____

10. According to research, what two factors influence children's view of death? _____

_____

11. How are children at ages two, six, ten, and fifteen likely to view death? _____

_____

_____

_____

_____

_____

12. What feeling do many children have when a parent dies? How can the surviving parent help the children cope?

_____

_____

_____

13. What are possible warning signs that someone may be contemplating suicide? _____

_____

_____

Section 21–2: Exceptional Children

14. Give two examples of invisible disabilities. _____

_____

_____

15. Do most children with a *learning disability* have below-average intelligence? Explain.

_____

_____

_____

(Continued on next page)

Family Challenges

16. Why do children with *dyslexia* have difficulty reading, writing, spelling, and doing math?

_____

_____

_____

_____

17. Compare *ADD* to *ADHD*. How are the symptoms similar? How are they different?

_____

_____

_____

_____

18. Identify two causes of *mental retardation*. _____

_____

_____

_____

19. What should parents do if they suspect their child has a serious emotional problem?

_____

_____

_____

20. Describe three traits often associated with *autism spectrum disorders (ASD)*. _____

_____

_____

_____

_____

_____

21. What are the educational rights of children with disabilities under the Individuals with Disabilities Education Act?

_____

_____

_____

_____

22. How do children with disabilities—and other children—benefit from the IDEA's policy of *inclusion*?

_____

_____

_____

_____

(Continued on next page)

The Developing Child: **Student Activity Manual**

23. Where can parents of children with disabilities get advice and discuss common problems? Where can they get financial aid?

_____

_____

_____

_____

24. Describe three traits that may suggest that a child is *gifted*. _____

_____

_____

_____

_____

_____

25. What do gifted children need to reach their potential? _____

_____

_____

_____

Section 21–3: Child Abuse and Neglect

26. Identify and explain the meaning of the four major types of child maltreatment. _____

_____

_____

_____

_____

_____

27. Give two signs that might indicate each of the following problems.
   A. Neglected child: _____

   _____

   _____

   B. Physically abused child: _____

   _____

   C. Sexually abused child: _____

   _____

   _____

   _____

   D. Emotionally abused child: _____

   _____

   _____

(Continued on next page)

Family Challenges   *Chapter 21 continued*

28. Describe three family situations that often seem to be involved in child abuse cases.

_____

_____

_____

29. Why does substance abuse often lead to child abuse? How are some *addiction counselors* able to help families?

_____

_____

_____

_____

_____

30. Who does the law identify as *mandated reporters*? What are they required to do? _____

_____

_____

_____

31. What is the purpose of *crisis nurseries*? _____

_____

_____

_____

32. How is learning about child development one way to help solve family problems? _____

_____

_____

_____

The Developing Child: **Student Activity Manual**

Family Stresses

Helping Children with Problems

Directions: Below are several letters written to the advice columnist of the local newspaper by parents who have troubled children. Read each letter and then answer it in the spaces below with the best advice you can give.

1. Ever since the divorce, my daughter, Jada, has been acting as if I make her life miserable. I can't figure out why, since she knows the breakup was her father's fault. Every Saturday morning, when he picks her up, she's sunny and cheerful. On Sunday, when Jada comes back home, she's grumpy and upset. Why is she taking it out on me?

_____
_____
_____
_____
_____
_____
_____

2. My wife's mother is dying of cancer, and we wonder what to tell the children. They're 10 and 12. They haven't seen their grandmother in a long time, but they were very close to her before. Should we take them to the hospital or not?

_____
_____
_____
_____
_____
_____

3. My brother just died in a car accident, and the funeral will be in a couple of days. I'm not sure whether to take my five-year-old son to the funeral or whether I should leave him with friends. All the family will be there, but he's the youngest. What should I do?

_____
_____
_____
_____

(Continued on next page)

Family Stresses   *Section 21-1 continued*

4. My husband and I separated two years ago. The kids seemed to handle the situation well, but now my fourteen-year-old, Kyle, has become very withdrawn. He hardly talks to me, and when he does, he's usually angry. Could it be a delayed reaction to the separation? What should I do?

_____

_____

_____

_____

_____

5. Our family is excited about moving to a larger city, but our 10-year-old has suddenly started complaining of headaches. How can we get him to relax and convince him it really isn't a big deal? The move will be a fresh start for all of us.

_____

_____

_____

_____

_____

6. My daughter Jema has a friend who is very ill. She's very upset. How can we help her get through this time?

_____

_____

_____

_____

_____

Exceptional Children

Living with Children with Disabilities

Directions: You are a professional counselor who has a radio call-in show. People phone you with their problems, and you try to offer suggestions for handling those problems. Examples of calls that you have received recently are shown below. In the spaces following each caller's question, write what you would advise.

1. My ten-year old has Down syndrome. The school system wants to put him in a regular classroom. I'm very worried that the other children will pick on him and tease him. The kids in the neighborhood are fine with him, but in regular classes, there will be others who don't know him. I don't want his feelings to be hurt. Should I fight this idea?

_____

_____

_____

_____

2. My six-year-old daughter has never done well with other people. She cries whenever she's in a new situation, and it's gotten worse now that she's started school. She hates to go out in the morning. What might be the problem?

_____

_____

_____

_____

_____

3. In many ways, our son seems very intelligent. He solves everyday problems easily. He remembers things we tell him. Yet he is far behind his classmates in reading and math. His aunt is a teacher, and suggested that we have him tested for dyslexia. We aren't sure. We don't want the school to label him as mentally retarded. What should we do?

_____

_____

_____

_____

_____

_____

Child Abuse and Neglect

Learning About Child Abuse

Directions: Monte Foreman, the television talk show host, is interviewing Jessica O'Brien, the author of a book about child abuse. Read the questions that Monte asked and then, taking the role of Jessica O'Brien, answer them. Write your answers in the spaces provided.

1. I would have thought that people who had been abused as children would be the last people in the world to abuse their children, but your book says that they're more likely to do so. Why is that?

_____
_____
_____
_____
_____

2. How do you think the Internet and other technology have contributed to the growing problem of child abuse? What type of abuse is involved?

_____
_____
_____
_____

3. You say that child abuse can occur without a parent ever touching a child. How can that be?

_____
_____
_____
_____
_____

4. What should an abusive parent do to get help? _____

_____
_____
_____

(Continued on next page)

5. What are some warning signs that might indicate that a child is being abused?

_____

_____

_____

_____

_____

_____

6. In your book, you say that a child's counselor will report evidence of abuse to the authorities. Isn't this an invasion of the family's privacy?

_____

_____

_____

_____

_____

_____

7. What should people in our audience do if they know a child who appears to be abused?

_____

_____

_____

_____

_____

_____

Child Care and Early Education

Study Guide

> **Directions:** Answer the following questions as you read the chapter. They will help you focus on the main points. Later, you can use this guide to review and study the chapter information.

Section 22–1: Child Care Options

1. Why might a family consider child care for their son or daughter even if one parent can care for the child at home?

_____

_____

_____

2. According to research, what three things do children need in their child care environment for optimal brain development?

_____

_____

_____

3. How is *in-home child care* similar to *family child care*? How are they different? _____

_____

_____

_____

_____

4. What is the main advantage of hiring a nanny? What are possible disadvantages?

_____

_____

_____

_____

5. What does having a *license* indicate about a child care provider? What does it *not* indicate? What additional information does *accreditation* tell parents about the provider?

_____

_____

_____

_____

_____

_____

(Continued on next page)

6. How is a *play group* similar to family child care? How is it different? _____

_____

_____

_____

_____

7. Compare and contrast child care centers and *parent cooperatives.* _____

_____

_____

_____

_____

_____

_____

8. Preschools typically provide programs for children of what ages? _____

9. How do children learn in a High/Scope preschool program? _____

_____

_____

_____

_____

10. What is the purpose of the *Head Start* program? _____

_____

_____

_____

_____

11. Give three possible options for child care that might be available to parents during school holidays.

_____

_____

_____

_____

_____

12. Ebony and Marcus are evaluating a child care center for their two-year-old. Write one question they should ask and one observation they should make about each of the following aspects of the center.

A. The child care providers: _____

_____

_____

_____

(Continued on next page)

B. The facility: _____

_____

_____

C. The program: _____

_____

_____

_____

13. In a home-based care setting, why is it important to ask if there is a substitute provider?

_____

_____

_____

14. List the following sources of substitute care in order based on cost, from most to least expensive: home-based care, family member, nannies, child care center.

_____

_____

_____

Section 22–2: Participating in Early Childhood Education

15. What are three ways that an early childhood classroom can be made comfortable for children? How do children benefit from this?

_____

_____

_____

_____

_____

16. What are *learning centers*? How do they benefit children in early childhood classrooms?

_____

_____

_____

_____

_____

(Continued on next page)

The Developing Child: **Student Activity Manual**   **179**

17. What is the purpose of the dramatic play learning center? What kinds of materials might it contain?

_____

_____

_____

_____

18. Identify five basic health routines that child care providers should teach. _____

_____

_____

_____

_____

19. What procedures should child care workers follow to prevent food-related illness?

_____

_____

_____

_____

20. Why is it important that playground equipment be suitable for the age and developmental levels of the children using it?

_____

_____

21. Why should teachers plan a variety of activities for children? _____

_____

22. Teachers should plan play experiences that focus on what four areas of development?

_____

_____

23. What might occur during *circle time*? _____

_____

24. When planning a daily schedule, what three kinds of activities should teachers try to balance? What is *free play*?

_____

_____

_____

_____

(Continued on next page)

25. What information does a planning chart contain? What does an activity plan add to the planning process?

_____

_____

_____

_____

_____

26. What are three questions teachers should ask when choosing materials for the early childhood classroom?

_____

_____

_____

_____

_____

27. In what four ways can positive behavior be promoted in the classroom? _____

_____

_____

_____

28. Why should teachers involve older children in setting classroom expectations? _____

_____

_____

_____

29. Evaluate whether the following method for dealing with a preschooler's behavior problem is effective or ineffective, and explain why: "Tori, you may play on the swings or the slide. You may not stay in the kickball game, because you keep hitting Jamie with the ball."

_____

_____

_____

30. How should a teacher act toward the misbehaving child when giving a time-out? _____

_____

_____

_____

Child Care Options

Evaluating Caregivers' Behavior

Directions: Read each of the descriptions of young adults below. In the space provided, write your evaluation of each person as a caregiver, including strengths, weaknesses and suggestions for improving those weaknesses.

1. Tameka has been a child care aide for almost a year. She is energetic and likes to lead the children's activities. She wants everyone to like her and puts pressure on herself to be the best child care provider she can be. Tameka does best with structured activities where there is a clear outcome and not too many distractions.

   Strengths: _____

   Weaknesses: _____

   Ways to improve: _____

   _____

2. Jason has six brothers and sisters. He loves children and wants to make a career of caring for them. However, Jason didn't do well in his child development classes. He found it boring to read about children. "I'm not interested in theory," he said, "I just want to be with kids."

   Strengths: _____

   Weaknesses: _____

   Ways to improve: _____

3. Casey graduated with an associate degree in child care from the local community college. She wants the children to excel and finds their differences to be a source of stimulation for her. She's excited to report to work each day and greets the children enthusiastically when they arrive. She likes children who, like her, have energy and enthusiasm. She has less interest in quiet children.

   Strengths: _____

   Weaknesses: _____

   Ways to improve: _____

   _____

4. Ben joined the staff of a child care center with a degree in art and a minor in psychology. He believes children need more opportunities to develop their artistic abilities, and he prides himself on the variety of activities that he can create for children to enjoy. He finds outdoor activities and routine care times tedious, though, and doesn't enjoy taking part during these less interesting periods.

   Strengths: _____

   Weaknesses: _____

   Ways to improve: _____

   _____

(Continued on next page)

Child Care Options   *Section 22-1 continued*

5. Melanie loves her job at the child care center. She has developed a strong rapport with the children and earned the respect of the parents. The children clamor for her attention and help. She likes guiding them to do the right thing but has a hard time disciplining them because she's afraid of causing hurt feelings.

   Strengths: _____

   Weaknesses: _____

   Ways to improve: _____

   _____

   _____

6. Jessica always wanted a job working with children. She loves their enthusiasm and curiosity. She enjoys reading to them and doing science projects. She likes taking them outdoors and planning activities they can use to improve their motor skills. One thing she doesn't like about the center where she works is the policy that calls for monthly meeting with parents. The parents always seem to ask her questions that she isn't prepared for.

   Strengths: _____

   Weaknesses: _____

   Ways to improve: _____

   _____

7. Drew loves doing activities with the children at his preschool, but he is not very organized. When he is thinking about the next day's activities, he has lots of creative ideas for effective learning. But when he explains the activities to the children, his instructions confuse them.

   Strengths: _____

   Weaknesses: _____

   Ways to improve: _____

   _____

   _____

The Developing Child: **Student Activity Manual**

Participating in Early
Childhood Education

Giving Advice About Child Care

Directions: Read each description below. Then write your advice on how to deal with each situation in the space provided.

1. Trevor set up learning centers in his classroom. However, the children in the language arts center seem constantly distracted. They keep looking toward the children in the active play area next to them.

2. Brianna is an enthusiastic child, but she often causes disruptions. She gets so excited while playing games that she knocks other children down. How can the teacher slow her down without curbing her enthusiasm?

3. The teacher said, "Put your things away." "It is time to go to the next learning center." As usual, several children began to cry. They didn't want to stop their activity. This usually causes the class to get off schedule.

4. Ethan has a severe cold. His mother kept him home yesterday but brought him back to the child care center today since his temperature is back to normal. He is coughing, his nose is running, and he has very little energy.

Careers Working with Children

Study Guide

> **Directions:** Answer the following questions as you read the chapter. They will help you focus on the main points. Later, you can use this guide to review and study the chapter information.

Section 23–1: Preparing for a Career

1. How is an *entry-level job* different from jobs at other levels? What is typically required to move from an entry-level job to another level?

   _____

   _____

   _____

2. How do the requirements for a *professional* position differ from those for a *paraprofessional*?

   _____

   _____

   _____

3. What are the advantages and disadvantages of being an *entrepreneur*? _____

   _____

   _____

   _____

4. Kristina's aunt says Kristina has an *aptitude* for working with animals and young children. What does that mean?

   _____

   _____

   _____

5. What information can you find in *The Occupational Outlook Quarterly*? _____

   _____

   _____

6. What kind of information can be gained from talking to a person working in a career field of interest?

   _____

   _____

7. What are three benefits of gaining work experience? _____

   _____

   _____

   _____

(Continued on next page)

8. Briefly describe what the following methods for gaining work experience involves.

    A. Internship: _____

    _____

    B. Job shadowing: _____

    _____

    _____

    C. Service learning: _____

    _____

    D. Work-based learning: _____

    _____

    _____

9. Identify at least five factors to consider as you analyze a career? _____

_____

_____

_____

_____

10. Give one example, different from those in the text, of a child-related career that fits each of the following descriptions.

    A. Works mainly with people: _____

    _____

    B. Works mainly with information: _____

    _____

    C. Works mainly with technology: _____

    _____

11. Tyler thinks his long-term goal is to become a pediatrician. List two short-term goals he could set that would help him progress toward that long-term goal.

_____

_____

_____

_____

12. Why is being a *lifelong learner* important in today's working environment? _____

_____

_____

_____

(Continued on next page)

Careers Working with Children   *Chapter 23 continued*

13. Summarize the qualities and skills that employers want in the following areas.
    A. Personal qualities: _____
    _____
    _____

    B. Interpersonal skills: _____
    _____
    _____

    C. Basic skills: _____
    _____

    D. Thinking skills: _____
    _____
    _____

    E. Management skills: _____
    _____
    _____

    F. Technology skills: _____
    _____

Section 23–2: Beginning Your Career

14. Identify four ways of learning about job openings. _____
_____
_____

15. What happens at a *job fair*? _____
_____

16. What is the purpose of a *résumé*? _____
_____

17. Summarize what should be included in each of these sections of a résumé.
    A. Objective: _____
    _____
    _____

    B. Education: _____
    _____
    _____

    C. Experience: _____
    _____

(Continued on next page)

The Developing Child: **Student Activity Manual**

18. Why is carefully proofreading a résumé so important? _____

_____

_____

19. How can a good *cover letter* help a job seeker? _____

_____

_____

20. What does a good cover letter bring to the attention of a prospective employer? _____

_____

_____

21. Give five tips for a successful interview. _____

_____

_____

_____

_____

_____

22. What are some ways you can prepare for an interview? _____

_____

_____

_____

23. Aimee is disappointed to learn that she didn't get the job that she had interviewed for. What should she do?

_____

_____

_____

_____

24. Daniel is trying to decide whether to take a job offer. Give three examples of things he should consider in addition to salary.

_____

_____

_____

(Continued on next page)

Careers Working with Children

25. For each area below, describe the skills needed for job success.

A. Communication: _____

_____

B. Relationships: _____

_____

_____

C. Leadership: _____

_____

D. Teamwork: _____

_____

_____

26. Tonya is looking for a new job. Her current employer allows five paid sick days per year, so Tonya calls in sick on the day of her interview. Is Tonya acting ethically? Why or why not?

_____

_____

_____

27. Rodney suspects that his employer may have to lay him off soon because overall store sales have been down. Rodney is thinking he might quit rather than wait for the layoff. How might Rodney's decision affect *unemployment benefits*?

_____

_____

_____

28. How will *COBRA* help Rodney if he gets laid off? Who pays the cost? _____

_____

_____

_____

Preparing for a Career

Your Interests, Aptitudes, and Abilities

Directions: In the spaces below, list your own interests, work-related values, aptitudes, and abilities. Be as thorough as you can. Based on your assessment, answer the questions that follow.

Interests:

_____

_____

_____

Work-related values:

_____

_____

_____

_____

Aptitudes:

_____

_____

_____

Abilities:

_____

_____

_____

_____

1. What kinds of tasks would you like to do in your job? _____

_____

2. Would you prefer to work with people, information, or technology? _____

_____

3. In what kind of work environment would you be most comfortable? _____

_____

4. What career fields do you think might be a good fit for your interests, values, aptitudes, and abilities?

_____

Beginning Your Career

Looking for a Job

Directions: Assume that you are seeking a job as a child care worker or another job that involves working with children. Complete your résumé in the space below by noting what you would include in each section. On the next page, write answers to the interviewer's questions.

Résumé

Objective: _____
_____
_____

Education: _____
_____
_____
_____

Skills: _____
_____
_____
_____
_____

Experience: _____
_____
_____
_____
_____
_____

Honors: _____
_____
_____

Memberships: _____
_____
_____

(Continued on next page)

The Developing Child: **Student Activity Manual**

The Interview

1. What are your strengths? _____
   _____
   _____
   _____

2. Why would you like to work in child care? _____
   _____
   _____
   _____
   _____

3. Describe a problem you encountered at school or in a job. How did you deal with it? _____
   _____
   _____
   _____

4. What rewards are most important to you in a career? _____
   _____
   _____
   _____

5. Describe an accomplishment that has given you great satisfaction. _____
   _____
   _____
   _____

6. Give an example of a creative activity that you would plan for our toddlers. _____
   _____
   _____
   _____

7. What sets you apart from other applicants? Why should we hire you? _____
   _____
   _____
   _____

The Developing Child: **Student Activity Manual**